Beyond the Comfort Zone: Building a Life of Meaning and Discipline

Jandiko

Published by Jandiko, 2024.

BEYOND THE COMFORT ZONE: BUILDING A LIFE OF MEANING AND DISCIPLINE

First edition. August 4, 2024.

Copyright © 2024 Jandiko.

ISBN: 979-8227090607

Written by Jandiko.

Table of Contents

Mastering the Balance

So much of life comes down to control: understanding what we cannot control while simultaneously capitalizing and making the most of the things that we can. A constant awareness is critical to our evolution. Epictetus wrote, "We must be at once cautious and courageous: courageous in what does not depend upon choice and cautious in what does." This idea has been shared many, many times in many ways over the centuries; another of which a lot of folks have heard is the Serenity Prayer: "God, grant me the serenity to accept the things I cannot change, the courage to change the things I can, and the wisdom to know the difference." But regardless of how it's said and who it's said to, the point is the same. There are things we cannot control, and we must find a way to stop exerting ourselves and exhausting our energy. They are, as the saying goes, what they are. These obstacles are immovable, and rather than continue to push and push with all our strength and energy, our time is best suited to learning to navigate them effectively.

Then there exist those things that are in our control. I believe it was in **The Power of Now** by Eckhart Tolle that he said, and I'm paraphrasing, "If something cannot be changed, stop thinking about it." The future represents anxiety—it's worrying about things that haven't happened yet. The past is essentially depression—it's worrying about things that already happened. We can't do anything about the past or the future; all we have is now. And if it can be changed, then act now to bring about the desired result. Take that first step and create some semblance of momentum, no matter how small. To worry about what is behind you or in front of you is actually insanity. I remember loving the simplicity and pointedness of that message: accept it, eliminate it, or adjust yourself to it.

Sometimes, it helps when I think about things in metaphors, and I tend to do it often. This morning, I was drinking coconut water, right? Of all things. And I was thinking, "Man, it'd be nice if those little pieces of coconut that float around in there weren't in there." So, I had this idea: just grab a strainer and pour it through the strainer into the glass. I'm leaning over the counter, watching the pieces of coconut collect in the filter, and I'm just thinking, sort of zoning out: imagine if those were my problems, just being separated from my life just like that; how nice it would be, captured in a little net and then discarded, thrown away. But it didn't take me long to realize a couple of things: One, such an idea would never happen. Life will always have some obstacles before us—that's what life does. After all, the word is predicated upon the avoidance of death. It's a struggle and a necessary one, which leads me to realization number two: we want hardship. Purpose and meaning are derived from our willingness to overcome adversity and transform because of it. A life without struggle is a car without wheels. Sure, you might avoid the fender benders, but you're not leaving the garage, right? So, that's a thumbs down.

So, I thought, what if I slightly adjust that thinking? What if it's a subset of problems that I can remove? That's when it kind of hit me: the opportunity at hand. Not the so-called problems but my thoughts about them. They're the real difference-maker here. The negative storytelling—that can be removed is pushed through the strainer. Again, it is not novel or groundbreaking. Like I said a few minutes ago, this idea has been around for thousands of years, but sometimes things land perfectly: right moment, right time. I knew what I needed to do was remove the worries and concerns pertaining to the events that I could not change, yet I exhausted my energy dancing around and around with my thoughts about them. You cannot change the future. You can change right now, which ultimately becomes the future, and there's a difference. I had to pull that back in. I think most of our problems are derived from anger or emotional attachment to the immovable, the unchangeable. One of my favorite sayings is, "You can't change the direction of the wind, but you can always adjust your sails."

When you remove the self-tormenting, you have going on about your past, things you wish you did or didn't do when you remove the concern that the future won't be exactly what you want it to be, which tends to be where I lean of the two, you're left with one thing: the present, right? Clarity. You have officially empowered yourself because the things you allocate your energy to can be changed, can be made better, or adjusted, and that's really what it's all about. You can't change the fact that someone you loved or cared about let you down, but when you dwell on it, you're now giving up the present as well. You're preventing yourself from doing what is required of you now to make your life better. You can't control the fact that your company is reducing its size and your department is being eliminated. You can't control the fact that only 8% get accepted to whatever you're applying to. You can't control the fact that you will be criticized for doing the unpopular thing, the thing that you believe to be right.

I say these things not to be a downer; I actually don't think there's anything sad about this. On the contrary, now that you've accepted these truths, accepted this as reality, now you can move toward what's best for you. No more dwelling on the unchangeable, no more fighting unwinnable wars. No, it's time to put yourself in a position to conquer whatever mountain is next. By straining out the things that cannot be changed, you are left only with what can. You can't change your company's personnel reduction, but you can find something else, something better out there. You can set the stage for a new journey. You can't increase the acceptance rate, but you can increase your value. Go above and beyond and put yourself in a position to succeed, and if you don't, they're losing. Continue learning, continue growing, continue moving forward. You can't stop the world's criticism, but you can learn to toughen up emotionally, trust your intuition and decision-making, and surround yourself with people you trust who lift you.

When you stop wasting time and energy on the wrong things, you get the right things. As Greg McKeown says in **Essentialism**, it's not what we can acquire but often what we cut away, removing the things that weigh us down, that we're dragging along with us everywhere we go. They don't need to be there. I say to myself often that I have everything I need. It's there. Some of it's materialized, and some of it exists as a seed that I need to identify and water and nurture, but it's all right here, which means the problem will never be that I'm incapable; it will never be that I'm not good enough. No, when I'm in the wrong, it's because I've forgotten to see it. I've either become consumed with the wrong things or lost faith in myself to do the right things. And knowing this has been a gift. It's been tremendous. It's helped me, even during the darkest moments, to reacquire what matters most.

Sometimes, it takes hours, days, even weeks, or longer, but I get there. Eventually, I will arrive, and you can too. You can parse out why you feel the way you do and categorize the thoughts in your head: Can I change it? No? Okay, gone. And with all that's left begins the journey. The good stuff. The adversity and the problems that will make you who you are. Please don't misunderstand me. I'm not saying it will be easy, but I'm saying it will be worth it, and that's critical to understand. Your world is there to maneuver and adjust, to reshape, but its transformation depends on a laser-like focus on that which is malleable, saying, "Do what you can, where you are, with what you have," will lead you to exactly where you need to be. Even if you don't trust the road before you, trust yourself to walk down it.

Embracing the Journey: Turning Somedays into Today

Today is not like any day I've lived before, and why should it be? This very second, there are roads to be explored that I've never before walked down. There are actions to take that I've never before taken and ideas to bring to life that I've never before given the respect they deserve. That said, my golden rule is that you are always one decision away from a totally different life. You are always one realization from pulling the lever, opening the door, and finding the answer you've been walking by all your life.

The problem is you don't see today as today. You see it as a continuation of yesterday, the same movie with the same characters and the same rules, without even realizing you need to change the script. Emerson said, "Write it on your heart that every day is the best day in the year." Why? Because it can be. Your job is to remember that things will continue on and on and on until we give them an end. We must manually close the book on yesterday's story and start anew because we can. We often don't realize it, but we can. And that is why the morning, each new day, is so precious. It's taking the mistakes and sometimes disappointments of yesterday and transforming them into today's lessons and the opportunity to begin again. A new journey was seen through a new lens, walked through a new pair of shoes, and a new sense of self.

So here is your reminder that the words "were" and "are" are very different. That's why each sunrise transcribes into the sky the hopes and dreams of you that you've always wanted to be. It's not a crazy formula or some secret code. It's simply untying your boat from the harbor that is yesterday and moving towards tomorrow's horizon. Someday, the things that you currently don't understand will make sense. Someday, the big things you're dealing with won't seem so big anymore. Someday, the doubts you have about yourself will be revealed as false. Someday, you'll see that the things you worry about don't matter at all. Someday, you'll see that the road before you wasn't something you had to walk flawlessly but rather something you had to trust and believe in. Someday, you'll look in the mirror and see that you had it in you the entire time, that there was nothing you needed or should have been hoping for. Yes, someday, that will all be true.

But what about some days from the past? I remember years ago thinking someday I would venture out into the world. Someday, I'd speak my mind. Someday, I would start my own business. I would surround myself with people who believed in what I believe. Someday, I'd make a little more money and have a little more time to do what I love. Someday, I'd have all that, and as I look around, I realize it looks a lot like someday. But guess what? As we grow, so do some days. It's a chase that never ends. There's always something more. There's always something bigger and better. The problem is not the ambition; the problem is forgetting that, in so many ways, you've dreamt of being where you stand right now. You have arrived. You're not the same person who, ten years ago, was throwing some days out into the universe. No, you have grown, you have learned, you have evolved.

Why does this matter? It matters because without acknowledging how far you've come; you cannot acquire the strength needed to go where you must go. When you don't feel good enough, it's often because you haven't looked over your shoulder and opened your eyes. The evidence is right there. It's hiding in plain sight. There's proof that you've been there, that you've faced demons and conquered them, endured your battles and overcame. You did that, and at one point, not that long ago, you couldn't say that you had. You weren't yet that person, but things are different now. What you have today was once only that hopeful someday. It was a fleeting thought; it had no merit and no value, yet you brought it to life.

Look what you've done. Understand how far you've come, how you ran when you could, how you walked when it was possible, how you crawled when you had to, and continued to arrive at a someday that is right now. You, my friend, are a maker of things unseen, an architect of tomorrows and some days. So don't you dare, don't you ever entertain the delusion that this gift suddenly stops now. Suddenly, the burden is too much; the mountain is too tall. No, what you do is overcome. That is who you are. You've done it for you, you've done it for the ones you love, and in some cases, the ones who didn't even understand that you kept going, marching through the fires of hell to turn some days into right now.

It is true that the road before you are uncertain. There's no way to know exactly how life will unfold, but that's beside the point. A bird can't predict every gust of wind it's going to encounter. It spreads its wings, takes off, and adapts because it can because it always has. After all, that's what it does. I'm not advocating that you should have all the answers. No, I'm suggesting that you trust yourself to find them, to move forward into the haze that surrounds you, to make sense of the seemingly illogical, and to bring about reality from the make-believe. Someday, you will have what you're aiming for, but here's never to let a day go by without realizing that you are always living out a someday from your past. You are always arriving and leaving simultaneously, the accomplished and the student, crossing the finish line and on the starting block with another race around the corner, another chance to stretch your legs and reach for the heavens. If you ever forget that, I ask that you find it within yourself to look over your shoulder, remember what you once asked for, and appreciate the journey that you have undertaken. You did that. Now, onward you go; you have more days to bring it to life.

Embracing Change: The Courage to Pursue a Fulfilling Life

———

I was thinking this morning about a conversation I had with my grandfather. In this particular example, I was living in LA at the time. My grandmother and my grandfather flew in from Boston, and, you know, I think we were doing some family stuff, but I wanted to hang out with my friends down the street. I wanted to go to Kyle's house, play Star Wars, and do whatever it was we were doing, and that felt like the world to me. I didn't want to miss out on that because I felt like I'd lose it if I weren't there; I'd lose something. And I remember him taking me from the kitchen to the living room and said, "Isaiah, you have to relax. That stuff, I promise you, will always be there. The fun, the escape, the metaphorical going to Kyle's house will always be there. You have to do what's right for you, and then when you need that, it's there." It was almost like all the nuance and details were requirable.

Why I'm bringing this up, and it's a little bit of a pivot, is because I've seen this sort of loss aversion throughout my life. Like I have mentioned, you don't want to leave a bad situation because you fear that the very basic boxes that you've checked, you can't get them back. You can have a job that you're not satisfied with, you're unfulfilled, there's nothing great about it, you've lost your sense of self and your purpose, but you're getting a paycheck. At least you have some direction in your day or your life. You can say who you are; there's some identity. There are some very basic boxes checked. You're not happy, but the basic boxes are checked. What you fear is if you leave in pursuit of something different, maybe you can't check those boxes again.

Or you're in a relationship, and it's not right, and you know in your core it's not right, but there are very basic boxes that are checked. You're not alone; you're with someone, and there's some predictability in your life. It'd be tough to lose those things. That's really the essence of what I want to say—having the self-belief and the self-trust because that's really what it comes down to, understanding that if you move into the unknown, you can recreate those things. You can check those basic boxes off. But if you don't dare to move out of that situation, you'll be shackled to a world that's not really meant for you.

The job thing—by the way, I always worry about saying this because there are people who love their jobs. I'm never, ever knocking a nine-to-five. It's just my thing, right? That was for me. I felt so constrained. I'm just such a—I love to be creating and sort of out on the fringes. That's just what motivates me. That's not how everyone works, so I don't want this to be interpreted as me bashing nine-to-fives. It's just my story. I realized that I could have walked away and come back in a year after living in, you know, Thailand, and things would have been the same when I got back. I could have got a similar job.

I could have found ways to check off those same boxes. Those foundational things are re-acquirable, just like the relationship thing. If it's not right for you, there are eight billion people in the world. Do you think one of those doesn't share your value system? One of those you can't have fun with, hang out with, relax, enjoy yourself, improve your life with? Of course, you can. But you're worried about losing the very basics, the very basic boxes that you've checked. You have to have the courage and self-belief to walk away from those things. You have to believe in yourself enough to know that you can recreate reality with a similar foundation but with the things on top that make you happy and make you feel alive.

Like I'm prone to do, I found a random internet quote today. It says, "I am learning to love the sound of my feet walking away from things that are not meant for me." It's that simple. You can never get where you're going if you're shackled to the things that don't move you if you're staying in a place of discontent. The message is simple: believe in yourself, trust yourself. **There's nothing in your life that you can't reacquire or rebuild**. But what you'll miss if you stay in that place is the opportunity, the upside, the people that will change your life, the places you've never seen, the experiences, the journeys that make life worth living. The upside is just too high. There's a quote attributed to Seneca that states, "No man is more unhappy than he who never faces adversity, for he is not permitted to prove himself." This means that it's in pursuing the difficult thing that we obtain meaning and recognition, that we prove ourselves. But prove ourselves to whom? This is the same Seneca who famously stated that we suffer more in imagination than we do in reality, that he is the most powerful who has power over himself.

That's one of the beautiful things about Stoicism—it makes us ask a very simple but often overlooked question: Who's really the adversary here? Who's the opposition we're dealing with as we fight our battles? What is it that must be transformed? Is it the outside world or the way our eyes view the outside world? What's really holding us back? What are the circumstances, or what are our thoughts about them? I think this is where we misunderstand the challenges before us. I want to delve into this power of perspective to explain that we are the gatekeepers between ourselves and our ideal lives. Very often, we do a good job of ensuring that the gate stays closed. We sabotage our own goals, dreams, and happiness while simultaneously pointing the finger at a million externalities.

When we look at the difficulties of life, and there's no doubt that life can be a very difficult thing,

it's easy to look at the world as this binary playing field: me versus the world. In fact, we often visualize the world as the enemy pushing back against us as if its motives were counter to ours. But so many of these narratives, these stories, they actually say nothing about the outside world. When we look deeper, it becomes apparent that they actually say a whole lot more about us. It's the one viewing that gets to decipher what the circumstance means, and so all narratives are reflections of the observers.

Jim Rohn used to tell a story about two brothers who had an alcoholic father. He'd come home drunk; he'd abuse his sons, and they had a terrible childhood. As they each grew up and had families of their own, their paths kind of diverged. One became abusive, and the other was kind and loving and caring. When confronted, the now-abusive brother stated, "Well, look, how can you blame me? Don't you see how I was raised?" But the kind, loving, and caring brother stated, "Of course I'm like this. I could never put my family through what I went through as a child." Same circumstances, different lenses, interpretations, which means different real-world results.

The idea here is to emphasize how one of the most important abilities a human being possesses is the ability to interpret the world around him. I think of us as subjects navigating a world of objects, as though the things around us don't have meaning until we place meaning upon them. That's what humans do: create narratives out of objects. That often overlooked, seemingly insignificant ability places a lot of power in our hands. Very rarely is it what we see; it's what we think and what we do about what we see.

Have you ever hung out with people who just tend to be happy, upbeat, and positive energy? I have a very good friend like that, where his first inclination is always to find the positive in moments, where I've sort of trained myself to pause, take a second, sift through the emotion, uncover the value in a tough situation, refocus, and take a strategic step forward, I look over at him, and he's already arrived there, right? He's been there for three minutes, right? Eliminated the negativity. It's his first instinct. He's the metaphorical kid hopping around in puddles, whistling at the top of his lungs while everyone else is hiding out from the rain or at least trying to find the courage to run out onto the street.

Then, some people seem always to find the negative. It doesn't really matter what the situation is; happiness is fleeting, only to reveal the negativity that never seems to go away, right? The kind of person that, if they won the lottery, their first thought might be, "Oh no, but what if I lose it all?" Both examples are people projecting themselves onto the world around them, the same way that smoke covers and consumes an entire room. It's not the room that's the culprit. Here's another example from Jim Rohn since we're on a Jim Rohn kick. He's making a similar point, and this is all from a collection of speeches he has on Audible, comparing humans to oranges, which is probably not a comparison you've made recently. But he said there's a consistency to orange in that it can be filled with one thing: when you squeeze an orange, orange juice comes out, period. It will never be apple juice or grapefruit juice; it will only emit what it has inside, which is orange juice. And while here's the connection: when life pressures us, challenges us, or metaphorically squeezes us, we only emit the emotions that are contained and available, that are alive and well within us. If there is no jealousy contained in our thinking, we're not going to project jealousy out into the world. If there is no hatred within us, we will not project hatred onto others. Why is that powerful? It's powerful because, again, it's one of the most important things you can do—certainly one of the most important things I've learned to do—is take that finger-pointing blame at the outside world, slowly turn it around, and point it back at myself, and ask, "What thoughts, what emotions, what ideas am I letting live inside my head that's altering the narrative, the story I'm telling about myself and the world that I live in?"

While one might think, "Well, that's uncomfortable, that's unfair, a little extreme. Why should I point at myself? It's not my fault," I would challenge you, at least for the sake of the next few minutes, to see such a change as empowering, as your advantage, as the bridge from where you are to where you want to be. See, if you always have feelings of, let's say, jealousy around a particular person—that feeling in your stomach like, "Oh, they have it all. They're ahead. They live how I want to live. They're this and that, and I kind of hate them for it"—you're naively giving the external world the power. You're saying, "I feel the way I do because of that out there, some cosmic injustice." You are powerless because you're neglecting your agency as a factor. But when you turn that finger around and say, "I only feel this way because I'm allowing myself to," then you can ask the question so many never think to ask: "Why?" Why do I feel this way? Which lights a path to "How can I fix it?"

See, the key to a better life is realizing you don't have to be in the passenger seat, pointing at and blaming the driver, complaining about the road being taken. No, you can get into the driver's seat. You can take the wheel. You can take control and inherit responsibility, and there's more at stake; there's greater vulnerability, but the upside is unfathomable. And I find myself thinking all the time, man, people are blaming the wrong things. They're shifting blame to the wrong adversaries. The real villain here is not the driver or the road or the weather. The real villain is the voice in your head pleading with you not to take the wheel, pleading with you to ride shotgun and complain as the world passes you by. And, of course, it makes sense to qualify that with the certainty that there are some things placed upon us that are just bigger than us that we can't control. You can make a list however long you want to—natural disasters, decisions and actions of others, and health problems. We don't often get to choose the landscape. So, as the Stoics would say, understand that.

Understand what you can't control and what you can because the beauty is that you can control how you navigate that landscape. And that is power. That is what makes the difference. See, the two brothers I mentioned a few moments earlier: same landscape, different navigational tactics, different views of what it all meant. One took the wheel, and one did not.

Accordingly, Seneca's quote states, "No man is more unhappy than he who never faces adversity, for he is not permitted to prove himself." Well, it's clear as far as I'm concerned. The question is not whether or not to face adversity. I think we all understand that. What I hope we take from today is a better understanding of what true adversity is, a better understanding of the fact that in front of us, there is always an answer, a key to every lock. Some people just don't think to look. They're so busy peering around every corner for external enemies and scapegoats that they don't permit themselves to succeed. It may be unfortunate, but it's true.

You can hit the bullseye over and over again, but if it's the wrong target, it won't do much for you. You might as well have missed by 50 feet. And I think that is what we overlook. You can't always fix the outside world. You can't change the unchangeable, but you can always change yourself. You can always fix yourself. As Tolstoy said, "Everyone wants to change the world, but no one thinks of changing himself." You're capable of being both your greatest adversary and ally, so choose wisely because the world around you will do nothing more than respond accordingly to your decision.

Leave the Old, Embrace the New

—

Just go. Sure, things will feel strange at first, abstract at first, wrong at first. It's incredibly difficult to separate from the past. It's hard to detach from the deeply rooted biological whispering of, "Hey, at least you knew what to expect back there." But that whispering has preservation in mind, not happiness, and at some point, we need to stop preserving that which is not ideal. So, go. The walls that once existed will crumble, and this will be startling at first, shocking at first, and intimidating at first.

It's incredibly difficult to watch foundational structures crumble around us, especially when you know you are the one who lit the fuse. It's hard to walk away from the faint murmur, stating, "Hey, this was your home. How dare you leave it?" But those words have status quo in mind, not growth. Home is an idea you take with you. It's no set of parameters. Just go.

The stories you told yourself, the narratives you thought were forever, will prove to be nothing more than the end of an underwhelming chapter. This will feel abrupt at first, unfair at first, and will leave you deeply unsatisfied at first. It's incredibly difficult to realize that happily ever after aren't linear; they're cyclical. It's hard to walk away from the voices pleading with you not to turn the page, stating that because their realities will remain the same, so must yours. But those aren't the characters with whom you'll emerge victorious. Some movies must be recast, the setting reimagined, and the hero reinvented. And so, it should be known that your greatest strength is the little steps that you are capable of taking, the little decisions you are capable of making.

Remember, safety is not safe when it keeps you from what you need, and the wrong now tend to evolve into the wrong forever. The small concessions, well, they become the big mistakes. So, if it's a sign you're hoping for, let this be it. If there's a time you're waiting for, let now be that time. If it's someday you are dependent upon, let today be that day. Doing nothing is, in fact, a decision but only one of many. One path laid out before you, one that single grain of sand where the edge of today's world touches the shores of tomorrows. Sometimes, it's about the ability to stand up, face the horizon, and just go. Go because it's only upon going that you realize you're capable of the journey.

You finally see in yourself the strength you've longed for. It's in going that you realize yesterday's situation wasn't even really the problem; it was your fear of the unknown, of leaving that situation. It was living with the devil you knew instead of potentially having to face the devil you didn't. That's what happened to your wings—they just felt safer tucked away.

But it's in going that we acquire perspective. The tragedies, the devastation, the things that kept us awake at night—they really weren't that bad. But how are we to know? When you build walls around yourself, what's within them becomes your entire world. It's in going that you create yourself, and while everything you need is already beating in your chest, the great unknown before you are the water to that seed, the key to that door. What you fear is exactly what you need. And so, the beautiful dance through life goes on—not beautiful because of its elegance (it's rarely that), but beautiful because of its promise, its malleability. It's beautiful because we get to move without answers in order to find answers. Beautiful because what we become is directly proportional to what we're willing to endure.

That means that the universe doesn't judge. It doesn't know us by our failures or our mistakes but by our courage. Our courage to face all of these things and move forward anyway, to relentlessly explore the resilience of the human spirit. An infinite light in an otherwise finite world, a bridge that is built beneath our feet in real time. What a weight off of our shoulders to know this. We don't have to get it right; we just have to step out the door, trusting that we will pick up enough pieces to put together something meaningful. We just have to go, and in the world, it opens up just like that. Leave the old, embrace the new. Simple, you think to yourself. Well, yeah, of course—the best things in life are always simple, always have been, always will be. We just imagine them to be difficult.

We have a knack for making simple decisions into complex matrices of cause and effect, pros and cons, and wins and losses. We learn to think for years until we finally come to the brilliant realization that happiness, that meaning, that a life well lived comes when we think less.

Ready, fire, aim. There is no perfect path, just an adjusted course, an endless series of changes, of learning that falling is just a road sign indicating where we need to go next. You can't plan for that; you can't chart a course that doesn't exist. No, you leave who you were yesterday behind, and you set sail. They'll ask you, "Where do you see yourself in five years?" and you'll think, "Who knows? But not here.

It couldn't be here. It must be somewhere evolved, where pieces of the world shaped your outlook and became the armor that you now wear." New game, new rules, new expectations, new people, new places. And what really changed? Well, how you view yourself. It's funny how it all works, how things come together when we look over our shoulders like they were meant to be as if this had to be the way things are. No, you could very easily have stayed dreaming, looking out that window, wishing you could leave, hoping for answers that didn't exist. And so, the complex now feels as simple as we meant it to.

We move forward, not knowing but trusting. And we look back with a sense of understanding and confidence that was built over time.

In the game of life, some people go and people who stay, people who build and people who don't. I'm not saying everything will be perfect or everything will immediately snap into place—how could I? But what I am saying is that in moving forward, we pull back the curtain on the opportunity that is available to us. We move from the physical limitations of the bodies we walk around in and towards the infinite power of the mind that powers them. We become who we were always meant to be. How do we know what that is? Well, not until we look over our shoulders, of course. So, go. Make your mistakes. Learn your lessons. Feel your moments of pain and your moments of bliss, your times of doubt and your times of certainty. Because in doing so, you will have done the very thing so few people get to do with their limited time on this planet: truly live. So, go. Just go.

Sometimes, it's what we don't say that echoes the loudest, what we don't do that has the greatest consequences, and where we don't go that ultimately gets us lost. I remember, as a teenager, applying to college. I was working on the admissions essay, brainstorming with my grandmother, and talking over possible topics and approaches. And she read me this quote that's sometimes attributed to Mark Twain, but that's beside the point. The quote states: "Twenty years from now, you'll be more disappointed by the things you didn't do than by the ones you did do. So, throw off the bowlines, sail away from the safe harbor, catch the trade winds in your sails. Explore. Dream. Discover."

I thought this was the perfect bridge to the next chapter of my life, the latest horizon, the newest adventure. I thought it was incredible, and it was. It was exactly what I needed, and so on to that next adventure I went. But here's the thing: as life unfolded, this equation somehow transformed from exploration and dreaming and discovery into the question, "Well, what am I supposed to do?" Somehow, without my paying attention, life turned into a checklist, a question I couldn't get wrong, a test I needed to make sure I didn't fail. It's amazing how quickly we forget the infinite breadth of life because we're focusing on the dotted line before us, the one we're supposed to walk. Sometimes, we're so fixated on what the expectation is that we don't ask ourselves where these expectations are coming from. Who is so significant and wise that they know what's best for you to a greater extent than you do? So that's an important question and also one you can lose in your periphery as you follow that dotted line before you. When you have a destination in mind—hopes, dreams, ambitions—well, that's an adventure.

When someone else has a destination in mind for you, whether this authority is imaginary or not, that's obedience. And sometimes, the greatest disservice we can do to ourselves is not to stop and think, not to stop and ask ourselves where we're going and why. Do you remember when you were a child, and you got into trouble? Sometimes, you get sent to your room. For me, this was agony. When it was punishment, I wanted to be anywhere but confined within those walls. I hated being sent to my room. And then, finally, the door would open. My parents would say, "Isaiah, you can come out now." I'd go outside, play basketball for a little bit, and then, often, I'd find myself right back in my room, happy—playing with my toys, whatever I was doing—not a care in the world. And it's like, what changed? Nothing but the context. Same me, same room, same toys, same whatever I was doing. It was, however, no longer a punishment. And I think this realization is worth exploring.

We may not realize it, and we may not even be able to articulate it, but I think we long for control over our lives. We long to walk our path. And in this situation, the path led me right back to where I was. Sometimes, though, the path leads us in the opposite direction, far away to distant worlds. The end destination is not as important as the fact that we chose it, that we asked ourselves why, that we believed in the answer, and that we immersed ourselves in its execution. So, when Mark Twain talks about the things that we don't do holding more weight in our hearts, it's because those things we tend to skip over are often the very things that breathe life into our souls.

We'll go to school to get good grades, to get a nine to five, to get a promotion, to get a mortgage on a home. But the audacity to open that photography studio, the nerve to think you could rent a van and travel the country, the delusion to think you could start that routine that will get you in the physical shape you've always dreamed of—see, we're lucky to have the things that we have. The quality of life we lead now far exceeds those that came before us. Life is convenient, incredibly convenient. But what is convenience if it comes at the expense of purpose, of meaning in life? Because that's what steers the ship. A crisis of meaning ultimately mitigates everything else. There is no exploration without meaning, and without exploration, tomorrow becomes a repetition of today, not an evolution of today. What's incredible, truly incredible, is that our purpose can be rediscovered, our paths redefined. How? By having a long conversation with, you guessed it, yourself. By putting the phone in another room, by disconnecting the Wi-Fi, and spending time with you. Something along the lines of, "Dear self, what matters to me in this world? Where am I going right now? Is where I'm going right now aligned with what matters to me in this world?" And sometimes the answer is yes, sometimes no. Great. But what we have now is a foundation to work off of, an awareness that you created that should be celebrated.

It's so easy to walk through life and never have that conversation. It's so easy to sleepwalk to the tune of someone else's song, the beat of other people's drums. But when you open your eyes, you see the correlation between your thoughts and your actions, your actions and your reality. You realize that when you wake up, that tendency to ask yourself what you have to do today, to reflect on your problems—those questions you assumed were normal, that you never gave much thought to—well, now you'll see you can dismantle that notion. Now you'll see that if you can ask yourself what you have to do, you can just as easily ask yourself what you want to do, what you get to do, and what life is inviting you to do. If you can reflect on your problems, you are just as capable of reflecting on the opportunity at your fingertips. If you can spend time dwelling on whether you're walking the obligatory dotted line that's been laid out in front of you, you're just as capable of redrawing that line and allowing it to pull you into a new dimension.

Listen again: "Twenty years from now, you will be more disappointed by the things you didn't do than by the ones you did do. So, throw off the bowlines, sail away from the safe harbor, and catch the trade winds in your sails. Explore. Dream. Discover." Explore, but for you. Wander down those paths that have piqued your curiosity for so long. Try things you once felt like other people were entitled to but you'd never permitted yourself. Be that for yourself because no one will come up to you and randomly give you that green light. Because without building your castles in the air, as Thoreau calls them, you live your entire life on the ground. You'll never hit targets that you don't create. And sure, there'll be a time when you will only see the destination. Great, that's life. But with each step forward, as it becomes more real for you, it will make sense to others as well. Trust each step like it is, in and of itself, a miracle, and you'll find in time that that's exactly what each step was.

Lastly, discover. Discover who you are and what you're capable of becoming. As Emerson said, "To be yourself in a world that is constantly trying to make you something else is the greatest accomplishment." To forge your path, build your own life, and stay true to your own heart is courage. So, sail away because you have the ability, because you are strong enough, and because the story you're about to write doesn't continue until you turn the page on today's chapter.

On the Edge of Breakthrough: Embrace the Power of Perseverance

"Many of life's failures are people who didn't realize how close they were to success when they gave up." —Thomas Edison. This is a quote I use when I've lost my way and when my frustration over the lack of a particular result overshadows everything. I don't think we realize how transformative these moments are. When confronted by them, we're presented with two options: give up or emerge better than we were. Not intuitive, right? It's not normal to think, "I know this is hard, but hey, I'm one adjustment away from getting it right, one move away from uncovering momentum." That's why, in such moments, I rely on others to remind me, and it's why I remind you now. To reiterate how small a push is required to get things moving simply. This is to remind you that you want this. It does mean something to you. And you know what? These are the moments you'll look back on with a tear in your eye and a smile on your face, and you'll be grateful you pushed through.

These moments, the darkest of nights, the lowest of lows, when we're lost, we're stuck, unsure—they are the ones that matter. So, shake it off. See the difference. The reason so many people turn around is because they don't know the secret, I'm about to tell you, the very same secret those before have passed on to me. You don't need to do anything but not stop. And if that seems too obvious or cliché, let me explain to you that it's in going that we're forced to find solutions, we're forced to become more. It's incredibly hard to stop an object in motion, but the question is, can you move forward when you don't have the answers when you're tired when what you've been looking for is nowhere to be found? Can you imagine what the other side would be like at that moment?

Looking back on your journey, knowing that where others stopped, you hung on; where the cost was too much for so many, you laid it all on the line. These are the decisions you have to make now. So, don't listen to that voice rationalizing, begging you to take it down a notch or return to the normalcy of yesterday. Let this message resonate; hear me: embrace the fact that you are always one move away from recapturing momentum, from finding yourself again. It's there; everything you need is there. Have the patience to find it, the patience to do what you do best. Find a way.

The Pillars of Progress: Vision, Discipline, and Trust

I'll never forget listening to Jim Rohn while taking a walk in the middle of the day. I needed to get out, decompress, rethink, and realign, and this message came through my headphones. He said, "We must all suffer from one of two pains: **the pain of discipline** or **the pain of regret**. The difference is, discipline weighs ounces, while regret weighs tons." I needed that. I needed that because sometimes we forget why. In the midst of the day-to-day trials and tribulations of life, we forget why we endure.

There's a strange dichotomy that exists because, you know, you can't measure discomfort that hasn't arrived yet. You can't identify regret that hasn't materialized yet. In a way, you have to make that tangible somehow. You have to know that the sacrifices of today deliver you from the anguish of "I wish" or "If only" or "Maybe I could have." I've heard it said that the human ability to delay gratification is what makes us so unique and incredible, but that doesn't mean it comes easily. So, as I walked, I became reacquainted with the trust that I had in myself, in the future, and the steps I was taking.

It wasn't that I'd reached some grand finale but that I permitted myself to stop constantly expecting one, worrying when things didn't go as planned, and feeling disgusted with myself when I fell short. This is, after all, part of a process. And if one stays the course and builds a foundation of discipline to guide them towards what they believe in, things will evolve.

We feel uncertain because new things don't have a precedent, at least not a personal one. And that feeling of, "I wish I knew" or "Had some predictability"—it's real, it's common. But if minimizing regret is what matters most, then it also means that we must have the discipline to walk steadfastly into tomorrow's unpredictability—a long-term, sustained discipline. One of my favourite interviews is with Bronnie Ware, who wrote **The Top Five Regrets of the Dying**. She talked about surrender, and how she mentioned it in her book Letting Go. I asked her, "Can you explain that? What's the angle?" Because of the way I look at life, there's always something you can do.

You can always improve your situation somehow. She basically said, "It's not about what you can control or what you can do; it's about putting yourself in a position to live the life you want to live and then letting go of that which you cannot control. It's about not worrying over external forces as you walk your path because all you can do in life is walk your path." That became the marker or the question: Am I walking my path right now? Look at it like this: First, a vision gives you direction; purpose keeps you excited and injects meaning into life. Second, discipline keeps you moving; it becomes the tiny steps that transport you through your pursuit of meaning. And third, trust in the process that you are here to give everything you have to give, and then the rest, as Bronnie says, must be surrendered. But the reason I bring this up is that all of it fits together like a puzzle, like three pillars of a Parthenon.

When people reach out to me all the time, they're upset that they're not as disciplined as they'd like to be. They're listening to the speeches, reading books, watching the videos, absorbing the content, and trying to improve, but nothing seems to get the engine going. I'm wondering, "What is your north star? What are you aiming for?" because as far as I'm concerned, it's impossible to be disciplined if you don't have a reason. You know, when Jim Rohn states that the pain is in ounces, well, there's an implicit comparison being asked, right? Compared to that top of the mountain that you'd presumably miss out on. So, if the mountain top is not defined, you're on a fool's errand. That's why I had so much trouble with my old career, for example. It's hard to be disciplined when there's no buy-in on the purpose.

Using my previous metaphor, its little steps, sure, but towards what? If you don't know, it's only practical then to look around and ask yourself, "Why am I taking them? Why not go drink with my friends? Why not stream this series on Netflix until 4 a.m.? Why not skip the workout?" You can listen to people on YouTube scream at you to do more, be more, and try harder all day, but without that peace, it will not get you very far. A vision, the discipline to pursue it, and a trust in the process. And you could say the same with someone who might have a clear vision, a dream, a perfect idea of what they want but never takes action, right? The discipline never materializes, making the endeavor just as meaningless. Things don't change until you take that big picture, that vision, and break it down into little things you can do every day. That's it. And isn't that amazing?

The greatest, most influential people—from the friends and family that inspire us to the greatest athletes and entertainers to our greatest thinkers, creators, and world leaders—all they do is do a handful of things consistently every day in the direction of something meaningful to them. A process that has been talked about since the beginning of time is the compound effect, as Darren Hardy calls it. That breakthrough was huge for me. The realization that I don't need to leap any mountain; I just need to ascend one tiny rock at a time. And that is not a superhuman ability; that is a single decision. So, here, the question isn't, "Can you be more disciplined?" Of course, you can. The question is, which few things are most meaningful to you? Which will you be focusing on every day so that they expand and inject value into you and the world? And then lastly, there's trust—sometimes the most difficult.

Seeing the unseen and maintaining confidence in that which is unknown is an incredibly challenging expectation in an instantaneous world. A world where things are immediate, feedback is immediate, messages are sent across the planet instantaneously, and goods and services arrive within hours. We have forgotten patience because it is disintegrating before our very eyes. We are a society of now. But the best things in life take time; they require that we hold up our end of the bargain and that we trust life will fall into place. Belief in a process that will come to mean more than anything that arrives in 30 seconds ever could: a vision, the discipline to pursue it, and trust in the process. So perhaps you're overdue for your midday walk, your little excursion into the soul, to ask yourself, "What is it you are moving towards? Why are you doing? What are you doing? Does it mean something?" If not, perhaps some adjustments will be made. Perhaps you've lost sight of that North Star that lights up our lives and illuminates the way. Take solace in the fact that life is not as serious as we make it out to be.

We don't live in a world of right and wrong, good and bad, yes and no, but a continuum—an opportunity to seek out and find the beautiful ups and the meaningful downs. To set our sights on the horizons that matter. See, when the little things feel too complex or burdensome, it's because the big things are misaligned. And that is a powerful idea to grasp. It's never that life is too difficult; it's that we have closed our eyes. So don't be fooled by those selling you reality as some problem, some obligation that must be dealt with. No, today is the greatest gift of your lifetime, and the same will be true every day moving forward. And to echo Jim Rohn, absolutely, it is a gift comprised of sacrifice and discomfort along the way. But that's a small price to pay for entry to the show, for the ability to embrace the mystery and embark upon the adventure. When you're pointed to the right North Star, well, the road feels less treacherous on your feet, and the hills are less strenuous on your legs. What we often deem to be a lack of preparedness, ability, or strength might just be a lack of alignment. So, adjust because this world, flexible and limitless, invites you to do just that.

It invites you to explore until you've uncovered your vision, to pursue it like nothing else matters, to sidestep the obstacles, invert the setbacks, and lastly, to find hope when there appears to be none. To set your sails, walk your path, run your race, and surrender to that which is beyond your control. And you'll find that with a vision, with discipline, with trust in the process, there is no situation or circumstance outside the scope of what's possible for you.

The Journey Within

———

The little e on the car dashboard reminds me that I'm pointed east as I sit at the red light, perpendicular to Ocean Avenue, staring out at the water. This is it. This is as far as I can go. There are no more streets or towns or cities. There can't be any more stops along the way, just miles and miles of ocean. It's interesting for me to think about all the changes I've made up to now—growing up outside of Los Angeles on the opposite coast, relocating again and again, sometimes very targeted, methodical moves, sometimes just for the sake of change. But I was always moving, always going. There's a saying that **wherever you go, you take yourself with you**. You can change the scenario, the circumstances, the surroundings, but ultimately, you can never outrun yourself.

You are accompanying you on whatever journey awaits. And it's often not until you run out of real estate and there's no more road or options that you're forced to look in the mirror and acknowledge that it is you who must change. It's you who must evolve and become the person that you need to become. And that can be a scary thing. After all, anyone can get in a car and head east. Anyone can point the compass away from the chaos of now and move away from their demons. But how many of us can find the strength to look those demons in the eye? How many of us can make ourselves bigger than what attempts to weigh us down? All of us can, but how many of us do?

Are we running to something or from something? Because there is a difference, and that difference is not small.

One of my favorite speakers, Jim Rohm, when referencing our journeys through life and our push to make more of ourselves, essentially said, "It's not what you get at the other end; it's who you become along the way." I think, like everyone, I've forgotten that from time to time over the years. Forgotten that value is not simply in going but in becoming, in the courageous little steps that accumulate over time. I had forgotten that the external world might inspire or excite, that change might invigorate the soul, and that the road untraveled might remind me of life's beauty. But these externalities are only as valuable as you allow them to be.

They're only opportunities if you decide them to be so. Change inspires, but will you let it inspire you to do that thing you know you need to do but are terrified of doing? And that road might remind you of life's beauty, but will you let that reminder be your invitation to share your beauty with the world, whatever that means for you? Can you be that vulnerable? Can you take that leap in the story of your becoming?

See, it is incredibly easy to look out at the world and pinpoint its flaws. All those little problems and imperfections tend to jump out at us. But can you identify what you need? Can you be courageous enough to ask those questions of yourself: What matters to me? What does a meaningful life look like to me? Where am I falling short? That is a conversation that needs to be had, and it needs to be had often. Otherwise, we will drive and drive and drive until we hit the water and are forced to ask that question because it's interesting that when we don't pause and make the changes that need to be made, life has a way of ensuring that we do. But when it's mandated by life, it tends to be a lot messier, a lot more chaotic, at least then when we make the decision ourselves. But either way, we cannot run forever. Either way, we must step into a new pair of shoes and learn to walk confidently with them into the night.

There are plenty of little mantras floating around out there, little pieces of advice. Perhaps it's best for us to weigh them each individually and see what meets our needs and fits our criteria. After all, life is not one size fits all. One of my favorites among these is to do one single thing that scares you every day, and I'll tell you why. Because when we become conditioned to turn our backs on all the uncomfortable things in life, we limit our prospects of a better tomorrow. It's synonymous with the seed refusing water, saying no to the very thing it needs most. And what should be noted here, one of the reasons it's so dangerous is that saying no is incredibly subtle. It's not some big event or explosion; no fireworks show occurs every time you walk away from what you need. No, it goes unnoticed. Again, one of the greatest challenges is quantifying what we don't do. How do you measure that thing you walked away from? Well, unfortunately, you can't. You can't, at least until you're staring out at the Atlantic with nowhere to run and no more escaping on the agenda.

You don't know until you're forced to pick the pieces up and make something of them. And I say this so that, hopefully, it can ignite that spark in your soul that you need most, whether you previously recognized it or not. I say this to remind you how much bigger you are than your problems and how you can transform all that exists around you when you transform yourself.

There's a certain inevitability associated with how we see ourselves, and I believe this to be true at both the personal and the societal levels. Anyone can look in the mirror and see the past, where they've gone wrong, how inadequate and ill-prepared they are. But the courage to look in the mirror and see strength, to both identify and understand one's shortcomings, but know that you have the power to do something about it, to know that the times you fell or didn't make the cut, they don't indicate that the endeavor was all for naught or unequivocally wrong. No, there is so much good tied into your pursuit, so much beauty and courage ingrained in your soul. But imagine. Imagine a life where you no longer run from the gaps but close them.

Imagine finding it in yourself to begin that hero's journey. And where you used to run to protect yourself, now you take the offensive to grow yourself. Where you used to avoid the possibility of failure, now you chase the possibility of victory. You can have that if you want to. You can be that if you choose to. Sure, you may never be able to outrun yourself, but you can always adapt yourself to be that person you always needed to be. Sometimes, we just need the reminder that we are strong enough, we do have what it takes, and that the thing that hurts us most in the short term not only saves us pain in the long term but also becomes what we live for. It is where we find our meaning. And so perhaps this ocean before me is not there to remind me of my constraints, that I have no road left, but a reminder of just how often we measure using the wrong metrics.

Perhaps I needed to see again that it's not where I end up but who I become along the way. That when the internal self-steps into the shoes it's been too intimidated to wear, that when the world within becomes the beacon, you need it to be, the roads and the stops along the way matter a little bit less than the eyes that process it all, that decide what it means, how it will be utilized in the game of life. And so yes, the little "E" on the car dashboard says that I'm pointed east. But as I sit at this red light, perpendicular to Ocean Avenue, staring out at the water, I know this is only the beginning.

Embracing Hardship for True Greatness

Everyone wants to be great. Everyone wants to be the best, the top, the one per cent. Or, as the saying goes, everyone wants to be a beast until it's time to do what beasts do. See, what life has revealed and continues to emphasize is that our most vital decisions present themselves in the dark of night, the chaos of the battle. They show up amidst our discomfort. We know these moments, the ones that seek to stop us in our tracks and turn us around. They are what must be prepared for; they are the gateway to excellence. So, let's look at the big picture for a minute—life in totality. Because consistently doing the simple, easy things, they're important. Consistency of that which is simple is the foundation; it's what we build the structure upon. But it is far from everything. Moving right along, we have the difficult things that push us to be more, that show us who we are, that hurt, that test us—the temporary storms.

They are the armor we come to wear; they're what prepare us to endure the trials and tribulations of life, like a muscle that must be grown and developed. But the difficult things are far from everything. Because lastly, we have our defining moments, the moments that put it all together. When the sky feels like it's falling, the body feels like it's failing, and the mind feels like it's dwindling, presenting the question: Will you do the hard thing when you feel like you can't do the hard thing? It's doing what's difficult when the situation around you are screaming at the top of its lungs, "You've gone too far, you've separated from normalcy, you are wandering into something that can no longer be deemed predictable or safe."

See, running is hard. But running when you're tired, when you didn't get a great sleep last night, when you don't feel good, when you're busy, when your schedule's full, when you have things to do, when you're in the midst of your workout, and your lungs are screaming for air, the cloud of pain is hovering over you as you make your way forward for no other reason than you told yourself you would—that's not hard, that's transformative. Going to the gym is hard but going to the gym when you don't want to, when you don't even feel like stepping into the car, when your mind is trying to rationalize a day off, when you're asking yourself what the point was, to begin with, that's not hard—that's transformative. Growing your business is hard, but growing your business is hard when you've experienced a monumental letdown when you went all in and were left empty-handed when you were chewed up and spit back out. Yet, you showed up and kept your eyes locked in on that win—that's not hard—that is transformative.

See, these monumental moments, the ones that break so many of us, that we've all come face to face with throughout our lives, they're not about easy versus hard; they're about doing the hard thing when it seems as though you cannot do the hard thing. The world is saying no, your body is saying no, and that chirping in your head is saying no. Can you separate yourself from that hurt, that anger, and that disappointment? Can you segment the negativity, knowing that you will do what you can to remedy this situation? But that life's curveballs can't stop you from moving forward for the simple reason that you won't let them. When life gets hard, you have to be harder—the one who gets bolder. You have to learn to surprise yourself. Here is what I believe to be the goal, the pinnacle. It's what I aspire to become: when life puts me through hell, to dig deep and find the emotional IQ, the awareness to know that right now is the invitation I've been longing for, my chance to level up.

So, you might be wondering what brought this concept to the forefront of my mind. And well, it was one of life's inevitable setbacks, and I had to look in the mirror and say, "I'm not going to think about the technical issues that just cost me thousands of dollars and thousands of hours of my time. No, I'm going to, one, learn and put parameters in place so it never happens again, and two, find the opportunity." See, when we build back, we tend to build back stronger. Clean slate, a new lease on life. Where can I be better than I was? Where can I pinpoint and capitalize on the value I once walked right by?

When we adopt this mentality, we become unstoppable. Someone on the outside looking in might say it's over the top, and it is. But so are the things that I want. They might say it's not that simple. Correct—running away from our problems is simple. I'm not about that life. They might say it's impossible to do all the time, to think that way every day, and perhaps so. But if we bow our heads and retreat every time life isn't perfect, we'll never attempt anything. I'm not aiming for perfection; I'm aiming for progress. Those who aim for perfection tend to spend the entirety of their lives doing exactly that: aiming, planning, speculating. Wanting more for yourself means receiving more rejection from the world. It means elongated valleys of despair; it means deeper treks through the heart of the vast unknown, across distant lands and through turbulent waters. It means doing the hard thing when the circumstances are what mere mortals call impossible.

At some point, we must transcend the versions of ourselves we once were. We must re-categorize and redefine the adversity we face in life. Be the ones who find something where others see nothing; find value in the seemingly valueless. Let us start from the suspicion that there is always a solution, and if there is always a solution, there is always a way to bring it into existence. Some will stop at easy—fine, let them. Some will stop at hard—great, to each their own. But if one dares to push further, to trudge forth into the night, they will be tasked with doing the hard thing when the circumstances are devastating. They will be asked not just to sail the ship but to sail it through the storm, not just to build the tower but to build as the skies open up, the wind blows, and the ground shakes. That will be the difference—that has always been the difference. So, what will you do when the time arises? Who will you choose to become?

Taking the First Step Toward Your Dreams

In his play **Measure for Measure**, Shakespeare wrote in 1603 a line that I think adequately sums up the reason so many of us fall short of what we are capable of becoming. He wrote, "**Our doubts are traitors, and make us lose the good we oft might win by fearing to attempt.**" Our greatest tragedies and regrets in life tend not to be our mistakes; they're not when we try, and we falter. No, the vast majority of the time, they arise when we do not even attempt because fear has prevented that very first step. It's when we have that perpetual light shined on all that can go wrong while the upside and the opportunity sit in the dark, just out of frame and in a world where you get what you focus on, to only focus on the worst possible outcome is a death sentence. It's debilitating.

The way I see it, there are a million ways to improve something. There are infinite roads and paths and possibilities. None are certain, but what is? Here's the interesting thing, though: the only certainty, the only thing that is for sure, is that if you don't go, you will not arrive. One will never finish what one does not start. Listen to this quote from Thoreau. It's from his book **Walden**, which he wrote after about two years and two months of living in the woods by Walden Pond in Concord, Massachusetts. He wrote, "I learned this, at least, by my experiment: that if one advances confidently in the direction of his dreams, and endeavors to live the life which he has imagined, he will meet with a success unexpected in common hours. He will put some things behind, will pass an invisible boundary; new, universal, and more liberal laws will begin to establish themselves around and within him; or the old laws be expanded and interpreted in his favor in a more liberal sense."

In other words, the world does not dictate; it reacts. It becomes what we decide it will be. And I was thinking about this recently. Have you ever thought about the utility of water, just water, and how it is obviously essential for life? Specifically, humans can't live longer than about three days without it, yet we can also very easily drown in too much of it. The same thing that's required for life can easily take life away. It all depends on how it's being utilized. When I think about this, my mind goes to Shakespeare's message on our doubts making us traitors if we let them, or Thoreau's passage about moving with conviction towards the things that matter, towards our dreams. What I see is an intentional restructuring of the world around us. The idea that life can work for us or work against us. It can be our headwind or our tailwind, the reason we stay or the reason we leave. And who decides that? You. You decide that.

I often think back to my first creative project once I took the entrepreneurial route years and years back. I referred to the project as **Quiet Desperation**, in reference to actually another Thoreau quote: "Most men lead lives of quiet desperation," because I realized around that time how easily that could become a reality and decided to do something about it. For me, it was a huge step out of the routine and the cycle. I finally asked myself who I was living for, where I lost myself or had simply never bothered. I want to find myself, but I don't know the answer to that. But I know at the time, if you asked me, "You know, Isaiah, what are you truly excited about?" it would probably be a lot easier for me to tell you about the things I didn't like, that I was afraid of, that I was unhappy with. That's what I saw, that's what I focused on, and that's the point. Until then, I was immersed in Thoreau's dreaded common hour thinking and so used to it that I thought nothing of it.

There was no next step or other side and then I arrived at that moment, that moment I hope we all get to at some point, realizing there's very little to lose and everything to gain.

It drives me crazy how hard we have to fight for this understanding and how much easier life would be if it were intuitive. But it's not; it's a journey, a muscle that must be built, and so we must build. We have to prove to ourselves that what's big and intimidating can be broken down and that what we visualize can materialize. That will always be true, but we need to make ourselves believe it. Identity is scripted; confidence is earned, not once but every day and we must understand the pain associated with staying far exceeds the pain associated with moving towards our dreams. The former is destructive, and the latter is what we need. They are not the same. You are so, being as we choose what we see, how about a commitment? Not a commitment to be perfect, not a commitment to have all the answers or avoid mistakes. No, how about a commitment to allow ourselves the courage to be imperfect, a commitment to go when we don't have the answers, a commitment to see mistakes as a necessity instead of a catastrophe? In this world of subjectivity, make sure that the movie playing in your head illuminates the opportunity, not the loss, so that when you fall, the inclination isn't to run from the bad but to look for the good. Because I promise you, you will get what you look for. That perspective will alter your actions, which will alter how you see yourself, which will alter the trajectory of your life. Let's leave that mediocrity, that common hour of thinking, behind as we head for higher ground.

Commonality, being average, it's a wolf in sheep's clothing. It seems simpler, sure, it seems easier, but the ones immersed in that world are depriving themselves of the answers they desperately need. They're refusing the hand that is perpetually reaching out. When we turn our backs on the extraordinary, it is because fear has gripped the wheel, and we are now passengers along for the ride. But you can be more; you can move towards what matters to you, take the steps one at a time, bear the discomfort one second at a time, and acclimate one day at a time. This is a journey dependent entirely on you and your willingness to step out the front door to see the things you previously disregarded. And when your eyes open, you'll see that you can be your ally or your enemy. This can be the beginning of a new chapter or the continuation of a current one. This is your story. And by the way, that doesn't mean others wouldn't love to make it theirs, wouldn't love to tell you that life is beyond your control, wouldn't love for you to think that you are dependent on the outside world, that you need them and what they are willing to provide for you. But no, this is about your understanding that the first step starts with you and your decision and that your autonomy is a strength and a chance to begin again. Change the way you think, and what you get changes. It's not magic but practical evolution. When we force ourselves to see the positive, when we look for a way, we find it. That's reality changing because you decided that it should and that's what the power of perception is: nothing more than unlocking the gate that was previously placed before you. There's no better time than this very moment to walk through it and rewrite your story as it should be written.

The Power of One Step at a Time

Here's an idea that's changed my life, as has been attributed to Nelson Mandela: the saying goes, "Everything is impossible until it's done." Right? We view impossibility as this abstract, scary concept, implying that something cannot happen, that it's not reality, it's outside the scope of what we are capable of doing or creating and we feel that. We feel that when we're in the middle of life's trials and tribulations, we feel that push-pull. You know, we feel that when we're working on something, and we feel unvalidated, we feel like everything's in vain like we're putting in time and energy. Where's a life rewarding us? Where is that, you know, the top of the mountain, the medal? Where's the applause? I cannot find it.

When we feel that, you know, the solution seems impossible, nothing short of impossible and what I want to do is kind of debunk that idea and show you how that abstract notion of something that just seems too big, it seems, it just seems impossible, how you can take that and break it down into very doable, manageable daily tasks that change your life and your relationship with the word. I want to give you two examples of books that I've read, but I don't think in this context, of how human beings have done "impossible" things and not even realized it until they stepped outside, right?

Until they crossed some finish line, some abstract marker, looked back, and went, "Oh my God," and the rest of the world went, "Oh my God, that's not realistic." And what's incredible is, as the impossible was being done, the steps to get there were so small and so commonplace that the people carrying out the impossible acts didn't even understand, didn't know.

They were just putting one foot in front of the other and so, both stories are related to war, and I feel like when you take sort of the darkest elements of humanity, stuff that's inconceivable to a lot of us. You see how people were able to get through those situations. It puts things into perspective. Right? We're not dodging bullets here in our world and that idea helps ground us. So, the first is Laura Hillenbrand's book "**Unbroken**," and Louis Zamperini is the main character in that book.

It's one of my favorite books. He's a track star who ultimately goes to fight in the war, and his plane is shot down. He goes to a Japanese internment camp and just endures hell, mental and physical torture. He's beaten, he's starved, he's isolated, just goes through a mental hell from camp to camp to camp, day by day, sometimes thinking he would die, really not knowing, malnourished, watching people around him die, getting beaten. It's an environment that would be hard for us to comprehend.

One part of this story really struck me. It's when, at the end of the war, the prisoners are set free, and he's talking to someone about the trip and looks back and says, "I'd rather die than do that again. I couldn't do that again." It's "impossible," and I don't think he used that word, but that's the implication, right? There's just no way. And it's like, even as the reader, as you look back, you're like, "That is not something a human being can endure. It just seems like too much when you look at it holistically." However, what the prisoners did was take it one day at a time—one awful, horrific, grueling, unfathomable day at a time for years. Then, when the point finally came, they looked back and realized that what they had done was unbelievable: one day at a time. It was just heart-wrenching; it was so powerful to have him look back on his journey and say, "That's impossible! I could never do that again. I would rather die than do that again." That's how hard it was; that's how traumatic it was.

Yet here he was, standing tall. Another example is in the book **Lone Survivor**. Marcus Luttrell is a Navy SEAL, and he's in Afghanistan with three other Navy SEALs who are killed in action. There's a point where he is by himself, bit through his tongue, with a broken back, mangled, and he crawls seven miles through the mountains in Afghanistan while being shot at and taking enemy fire. The portrayal of just slowly moving your body forward, inch by inch to safety, again is unfathomable; that's impossible. That's not something we can comprehend. I don't even think it's something he can comprehend, and I'm certainly not going to speak for a Navy SEAL. But the idea is—it's just unfathomable.

One step at a time, one movement at a time, you can create a different reality. So, when you take these examples and pull them back down to earth, Viktor Frankl talks about in his book how suffering is like a gas that will fill any room. Everyone's suffering consumes them to some extent. You may not be at war, but we are all fighting our own battles. When we are in the midst of difficult times, it's easy to not think about getting to tomorrow but to think about surviving the whole metaphorical war—not just crawling one foot but looking at the seven-mile marker and thinking it's outrageous. So much of life is convincing yourself to move forward one step. It's such a trivial thing to discuss; it's not sexy, it's not, on its face, heroic or exciting. It's the mundane compounded over time, and we need to remember it most when it's hardest to understand. I talk about it all the time—that Nietzsche quote: "Those who were seen dancing were thought to be insane by those who could not hear the music." It isn't easy to stay fixated on a result that is not there. It's one of the most challenging things about changing your life and the world around you. You know, dreaming is putting things on Earth that are not yet on Earth. That takes mental fortitude because each step you take, you have to remind yourself that it's for something—that it means something.

When you desperately want applause, because look, it's human—you exert yourself, you exhaust enough energy, and any rational person is going to say, "Why the hell have the stars not aligned yet? I don't understand what I need to do." That's what's interesting: people don't talk about the fact that it makes more sense to quit than to carry on. To the rational brain, it makes sense that we would say, "No more! I want to deal with the world that I'm in, not one that isn't built yet." But it's why we celebrate. We celebrate those times when we move forward anyway, and we have the vision to see the unseen and do what so few people can do. That's what makes life beautiful; that's what makes human beings beautiful.

We see life through stories, and the ones that can write and craft narratives that have not been heard, watched, or explored—that's magic. I talk about the evolution of insanity. I wrote about this years ago, and it continues to be one of the most important things I think I've written. If you take a woman who leaves her everyday life; for example, and she has this passion, this sense of purpose, and she wants to breathe life into it, she leaves her ordinary world and starts building. She becomes obsessed with this idea, and people around her—by the way, who know her as what she was and what she did—they know her based on what they saw yesterday. They say, "This is weird," but she's locked in. She gets up, makes it her focus in life, and continues forward. Nothing happens.

People point to her and say, "Look at her, wasting her time! She had it all before; this is crazy." But she continues and continues, builds and adjusts, throws her understandings, knowledge, and experiences against the wall, and when they shatter, she picks them up and builds again and again. People say she's delusional; she's insane; she has lost her mind. But she hangs in and dances without the music long enough to get there. So wherever "there" is, she gets there. Now, the perception's different; now, it's exciting. Now, she's not insane to the world around her; now, she's propped up on a pedestal. People want what she has; they want to understand how to build what she built. They want to know how they can do what she did. They call her lucky. She says, "No, for you to call me lucky is insane."

What she did was build the impossible with very ordinary, very mundane steps—never losing faith and remembering, and this is the key concept: remembering that all those little trivial steps mean something. When she steps outside, because we all get there, we will step outside and look back and reflect. We'll look back on the impossible that we built, on the magic we created. The thing is, we need to remember that magic is manufactured with very real, practical components of life—simple decisions. It's like the human brain is so much more than the sum of its parts. You can take any element of the human brain, and it doesn't seem that extraordinary. We can't even explain or understand it. But you put it together, and we have something that transcends the biology and the physicality that we look at under a microscope. It doesn't make sense; we haven't quite figured it out.

All those little pieces become something meaningful. My point is that we all have our journey. We're all fighting our own battles. We're all going to get to a point because it's human and, in a way, required, where we look around and question ourselves and the process. We don't know if it's worth it; we forget why we started. We can't see the finish line because it's not there yet, and we'll only see it if we continue to uphold that vision in our heads. That's when it's important to remember what impossible is and how it's made—every simple decision to step forward in crafting the impossible. I had a call with someone today: a very successful individual—right, a very skilled and respected person in his field, a brilliant platform, a great communicator, and just an all-around impressive human being. He says, "Yeah, but I want to be one step further. I'm getting frustrated. I don't know what can I do to get there?" It's like I've been in that spot. In fact, I find myself there a lot, and I think it's incredible that you're looking out and asking, "What pivots can I make? What adjustments can I make?"

But sometimes, what you don't do is more important than what you do, and what you shouldn't do is lose sight of how much you've built. What you shouldn't do is forget that one step at a time creates miracles and that you are well on your way to where you want to be. Yes, ask that question: "How can I evolve? How can I level up?" But never let impatience trump the big picture—never at the expense of who you are and what you've made.

Sometimes, life is about just moving forward. Sometimes it's about the trivial; sometimes it's about the mundane. That's what hurts; that's what gets you. Most people don't quit because of a traumatic experience. Most people don't quit because they took a monumental loss; they quit because the little things don't reveal their value. It's very hard amidst the chaos of day-to-day life to remember what you're building, to remember each little step is a brick that will evolve into the impossible. Dance before the music plays. Believe in the song, believe in the melody, and believe in yourself because there will be a point where you get there.

It is a very abstract thing, and it means many different things to many different people. But there will be a point when you arrive. You'll exhale, look back on what you've done, and be thankful. So, wherever you are, when you lose sight of your journey, think about that moment. Think about how that will feel—looking back on what you've made and all those times you could have stopped and didn't, all those times you wanted to say no, but you said yes. They mean something; I'm telling you; they mean something. But that is not half as important as the fact that you know it means something. You just need to remind yourself of that fact. So, here's to one step more in building the impossible.

Unleash Your Inner Lion

What if I told you that you already know what must be done? You just need to put yourself in a position to do it. You need to unlearn the rules that crippled you, the ideas that confined you. We are in constant pursuit of the thing that will magically right all our wrongs, the answer that will give us something we've never had. Know that everything you need, you have now; you just need to allow it to flourish. Declutter, simplify, remove all that unnecessary stuff, and walk your path. Einstein once said, "Everyone is a genius, but if you judge a fish by its ability to climb a tree, it will live its whole life believing that it is stupid." What's great about this is the idea that who we are is not found; it's acknowledged, it's accepted. In our world, there are so many fish, as Einstein says, trying to climb trees, which creates a sense of learned helplessness. We are judging ourselves using the wrong metrics, equipped with the skills, characteristics, and abilities to win in our arenas but playing in someone else's. How loyal are you to your instincts? Do you do what you know is right or what you feel obligated to pursue? When was the last time you listened to me? In Tim Grover's **Relentless**, he introduces a brilliant metaphor. He says, "A lion doesn't have to be taught to be a lion; it just is. It hunts, runs, roams, explores, and lives life the only way it knows how." Now, if you capture a lion, bring it to the zoo, or put it in a cage, it will carry itself differently. It will lie down, move around lazily, and sluggishly navigate its little space. To passersby, they'd never know what that lion really is; they would never know what it looks like in its element. But despite all this, it is still, in fact, a lion.

It maintains that killer instinct; its characteristics haven't disappeared. If it were released from the cage, it would go right back to doing what lions do—being what lions are meant to be. It just has to ditch the cage, and the point is perhaps so do you. There's a little light in your soul that waits day and night to explode into something meaningful, where your nature meets your environment. Where the "I shouldn't do this," the "odds are impossible," the "I'm not good enough," and the "I can't lose what I have now" all fade away, where it's left behind you, and you're finally free to reign over your territory, your own life, your empire.

See, we constantly feel like our glasses are empty, like we're missing pieces, in need of something—just one more thing that will be our answer. That's all we need. I can say with confidence it's not about what you need; it's about what you no longer need. It's about mitigating the noise so what matters can shine through—removing those people in your life that drag you down or add no value. It's about getting rid of the things that make your world unnecessarily complex, removing the need for immediate validation, success, and accolades, and instead embracing the little hinges in your life that W. Clement Stone said will ultimately swing the biggest doors.

We all have the lock, the key, and the map right there amidst the trivialities of our day-to-day, and we walk right by them, look right at them, pick them up, and put them down. But have we learned to see them truly? Everything starts with that awareness. My life did not change until I recognized that and began asking myself questions, I'd never asked before—big-picture questions, obvious questions. But just because it's obvious doesn't mean it's always intuitive.

What do I want out of life? What is important to me? What's something I love doing that I can dedicate myself to and that I can commit to being great in the long term? That I'm so immersed in that when the inevitable downtimes arrive—the losses, when the doubt and insecurity creep in—I can keep moving forward because I'm so in love with the process. But I don't let the little things define me.

As Jordan Peterson famously puts it, "Choose your sacrifice." A life of meaning isn't easy, but there's nothing more fulfilling because when you embark upon that journey, it allows for the evolution of the self. We can become something more. Nietzsche says, "Those who have a "why" to live can bear almost any how." We equip ourselves for anything the universe can throw at us. We position ourselves to evolve. Viktor Frankl says, "Man's main concern is not to gain pleasure or to avoid pain, but rather to see meaning in his life." To align yourself with and pursue that which is your reason for living—that's how we transcend the day-to-day life we've come to know. When we breathe in possibility, dance with the infinite, and, of course, something of this magnitude consists of ups and downs. It's not an easy road, but it's the one worth taking.

Our metaphorical lion doesn't succeed every time he's prowling for food, but he doesn't roll over and die. He doesn't recede or quit being a lion; he gets up tomorrow and does it again because it's who the lion is. And while life doesn't unfold until you find that same thing for yourself, people say, "Well, I don't know. That's the problem." That's not the problem; that's the essence of life. That's the beauty—you're here to explore and find that for yourself. But the power is knowing you're not looking for something or someone to save you; you're looking for an environment in which you can best be you. You're looking for the right terrain to share your gift with the world. If you have what you need, then you're not looking for the product; you're looking for the delivery mechanism, the vehicle to nurture and transport your value to a world that desperately needs it. You're looking to build yourself up and, in the process, amaze yourself. Look—what you're capable of is beyond comprehension, limitless, almost unfathomable, but it is, as Ryan Holiday says, a confidence that must be earned. So, start now, earn it. Let yourself succeed.

Your intuition knows what feels right and what doesn't, but the seed must first be planted. So, make today about setting yourself up for success, turning off the idea that you're one piece away from completion, one minute away from starting. No, you are ready now. You have what you need now. You know what's necessary now. You just have to be your ally, put yourself in a position to be yourself, let your values shine, and double down on what matters to you. Look, it's not a game of acquisition; it's a game of courage. Do you have the courage to be who you are, to follow that potential, that possibility into the great unknown?

The Power of Perseverance

S ometimes, what we need most is not what we think we need most. It's not that break we've been waiting for the universe to provide or the answer we've been desperately seeking. No, sometimes we need only three words: **don't give up**. Don't turn back now and see, I know you want to, and that the meaningful thing, the right thing, requires we give all of ourselves. It's metaphorically speaking the most exhausting, sometimes disheartening, but this is your reminder that there will come a point when you look back on this moment, and the best thing you'll have ever done will have been continuing to put one foot in front of the other, continuing forward despite the circumstances, towards that which means something to you.

I remember in South Florida a handful of years ago, I just moved down here and was exploring the area a little bit, looking for a place to live. I found this kind of odd little park in between a parking lot and the beach, pulled over, and just started walking around. I ended up sitting down on this bench that faced the ocean and just looked out for a while. I remember looking at the people who all seemed so happy and fulfilled like they had it all together. I looked at the ocean that was so much bigger than me, so vast, so powerful, at the non-stop stream of planes flying overhead that all seemed to have a direction, a purpose; they had their courses mapped and I think I remember it so vividly because I'd never felt more alone than at that moment, like deeply, painfully alone.

It's not that I enjoy bringing up these types of experiences; I bring them up because time has repeatedly revealed that from these moments of doubt and sometimes even despair come what we need most, so long as we don't run from what the world is trying to provide us. It's as though we must experience emptiness before we can become fulfilled. We need to be overcome with this sensation that there's no way out before realizing that there is always a way, so long as we're willing to find it. And the pain associated with that willingness—well, it far outweighs the alternative.

I often break things down into this dichotomy of the easy, meaningless way versus the hard, meaningful way, but that may be oversimplified. Easy compared to what? Hard compared to what? It's easy to shut down when we're at our lowest; it's easy to stop when it hurts. But easy now evolves into what's actually incredibly difficult tomorrow—a difficult, heart-wrenching, regretful forever.

Admittedly, he is a controversial figure, but regardless, one of the most important quotes I've ever read was by Lance Armstrong in his book It's **Not About the Bike**. He says, "Pain is temporary. It may last a minute or an hour or a day or a year, but eventually it will subside and something else will take its place. If I quit, however, it lasts forever." See, the easy thing versus the hard thing is too simplified and void of imperative context. The question is, in our darkest moments, will we stand up when it hurts so that we can walk, run, and ultimately sprint towards what matters?

There's a realization that helped me because when we're in these situations, the thought goes like this: things are wrong, things are broken, my life isn't what it should be, I need to fix this and make it whole, make it right so I can live a good life like everyone else. There's a deep loneliness associated with that misconception, as though the world is put together, but I am not. Well, let me dispel that notion and end that narrative.

The world is a series of objects that mean nothing other than the value we place upon them. Seven billion people, all fighting their own battles, all trying to make sense of things, all pretending like the little fairy tale they've manufactured in their heads is the real thing or the right thing when, in actuality, we are all just passengers along on a ride we do not understand, fighting battles that we don't often comprehend and cannot grasp. You are not broken; you are human, perfectly imperfect, and equipped with the tools to take another step forward despite the chaos and the uncertainty. Steps that become, in the end, everything.

I remember reading about Jefferson and how he had migraines so severe while president that he would do most of his important work in the morning because of the high probability he could literally be incapacitated from noon on. And

I just thought, man, we are all fighting battles. We're all doing what we can to make the most of our circumstances, to redirect discomfort into opportunity and pain into progress. And what's most incredible is that we can. There's a saying that it's not supposed to be easy. Getting where you need to go requires the treacherous path associated with a hero's journey, the vast unknowns, the questions that remain unanswered for extended periods of time, and the villains that seemingly inject themselves into our lives. Please understand that this is not a reflection of you, who you are, and your capabilities. This is the game of life. This is today's difficulty in exchange for tomorrow's meaning—the pressure that creates the diamonds. You don't have to be sure of anything other than that you know you will continue stepping forward because you can.

Things won't always go right, but in the failures are the new tools to grow and redirect. You won't always feel on top of the world, but it's in the valleys of despair that we're forced to truly analyze, think deeply, reapproach, and perhaps most importantly, you may have days where you let yourself down, fall short, or perhaps lose sight of the courage to which you have attached your dreams. But that's okay. You are defined not by your mistakes but by the present moment—not some impossible expectation of perfection, but by your ability to rise and rise again when it requires all of you to lift your head and carry on.

So go into that unknown, where fear is transformed into courage and doubt into strength. Go, because if not here, where? And if not now, when? All you need, you have. And when life finds you sitting down on a park bench, staring out at a world that feels too big and too complex and seems impossible to navigate, find it within yourself to smile. Smile because of what you've already overcome, what you've been through, who you are. Remember that you are here you need to be, staring up at the meaning of life as opposed to down at your feet. Now go. There are no miracles here; no mountains need to be jumped or oceans crossed. But if you won, step forward, and two, believe in yourself to put the pieces together as they arrive. There is nothing you can't do or be. No obstacle before you is insurmountable. Just keep going, and sure, sometimes that's all we can do but it also happens to be true that it is your greatest superpower—to simply find a way to run if you can, crawl if you must, but find a way because deep down in your soul, the pieces are there, and it will be, at some point as you look back, the greatest decision you've ever made.

Hold the Vision, Trust the Process

Hold the vision, but trust the process—an idea that should act as our North Star as we make our way through life. It proposes believing in a goal but, at the same time, understanding that its manifestation will be unpredictable and challenging. It may not unfold the way we thought it would. To me, though, the most challenging aspect of personal growth, of building the things that matter, creating realities we dream of, is the mandatory dance we must do with time—the patience that's woven into the equation. It's the empty spaces that we tend to use for manufacturing doubt and disbelief when life has given us nothing to react to. It's like we create monsters in our heads and it's really an incredible thing when you think about it.

I look back on the hardest parts of my life in the past decade, and some were excruciating. They were pain derived from what I knew I hadn't yet accomplished. It was feeling like I wasn't moving fast enough, like the winners in life had that over there, and all I had was this over here—a completely nonsensical narrative, but one that certainly felt real. Discomfort from the delta, or the gap, between what I wanted and what I had—a feeling that would randomly dip in and out of my conscious mind as I sort of chipped away at my goals day in and day out.

I started to wonder how I could better position myself to grow, to maintain that ambition, but also to do it with less anxiety. As I stated a few seconds ago, I want to hold that vision but perhaps improve my trust and relationship with the process—my ability to immerse myself in various pursuits without dwelling on the fact that I haven't yet arrived. I know this game; we all know this game. There's always going to be another finish line to cross. That's a great thing, but it can also, when we're not looking at it correctly, be to our detriment.

There are always higher numbers to achieve—again, an incredible opportunity, but with the wrong perspective, dangerous. If you can't find a way to appreciate the now while you climb, you will be forever lost. There will always be a hole that's never filled. I think we need to be better about supporting ourselves along this journey. No one can be there for me like I can, and I think that's true for everyone. We need to be our greatest allies.

Therefore, I brought this question up, as I tend to do, with a few of my friends, right? With different perspectives, they look at the world a little differently. I basically asked, "How can we get out of our own ways?" Or, "How can we both be tenacious in our pursuit of evolution, continue doing the things that excite and challenge us, while also being a little easier on ourselves, trusting that dance we do with time as the process unfolds?" I present this question to one of my friends sitting across from me at the table, and he thinks about it. He says, "Hey, well, that's what's got you where you are. That feeling like there's always more—it's the reason for the success you've had and the success you'll have in the future. It's what will push you; it's why you will succeed." People who accomplish things are never satisfied. Jordan was never satisfied; he was never happy. In that context, greatness and happiness are not compatible.

I took it in; I certainly appreciated the perspective. In many ways, I think he's right. It sorts of reminded me of the idea behind Tim Grover's book **Relentless**—that it's an obsession that must take place. It doesn't leave room for much else. Right? It is incredibly valuable to understand, if anything, just to see, just to grasp what it means to achieve in a world of obstacles but truthfully, I wasn't entirely satisfied. How can we better visualize the process so that we're more powerful allies to ourselves? That's what I wanted to understand. A short time later, I'm at the kitchen table, kind of going over some analytics for social media, like YouTube channel, podcast stuff, and so on.

My father, who happened to fly in from Boston, is at the kitchen table with me. We're having some coffee, and I commented on the trajectory of the numbers. I forget that particular week; maybe it was higher or lower than expected. I don't really remember. But he made this comment about the patience that I've had with the channel over the years—just an offhand remark. He said, "The numbers are like the S&P 500, right? The stock markets. There are days when it drops or days when it rises, but over the long haul, it's steadily pointed up, and it continues to point up." I found that so interesting.

I harp on the small things a lot on this book—the little breakthroughs that pave the way for larger transformation, ideas that change the way we look at things, which ultimately change the way we act, which change the results we get. And this happened to be one of them. It hit me just right: what is perhaps the most important piece in the famous book **The Intelligent Investor**? What is the idea that made Buffett a billionaire? It's that you invest in things you believe in, and you remove the emotion. You hold the dips. Right? When the stock market takes a hit, and everyone's panicking, acting emotionally, and selling, you don't sell; you buy more. Right? When the world emotionally rushes out, you rush in, and when the world emotionally rushes in, you step out.

Well, in life, there will be days when your metaphorical stock drops. At least you feel like it does, right? Those YouTube numbers, perhaps numbers in the old bank account, may cause fitness goals to fall flat—maybe you're just not seeing a return on investment but we are never defined by the events of the day, even the worst of days.

They're merely a small part of a much larger pattern, and the truth is, sometimes success is so small you can't see it. Of course, you're going to be anxious if you think every day should be comprised solely of mountaintops and finish lines. If you're always looking, comparing, contrasting—but sometimes success is 0.00001% better. Sometimes success looks like the S&P 500 taking a hit, dropping for a day, a week, or a month. Sometimes, growth doesn't look like what we want growth to look like. But just like intelligent investors, you are putting your money in the belief that at a certain point down the road, the value will be higher than it is now. This idea has been everything to me, particularly on the days when it feels like things are going backwards, over periods where I feel like I've been standing still, where the voice in my head is presenting all kinds of scenarios that I could have been better or done more. And maybe so, but these times are nothing more than data points; they are steps along the way.

Knowing this frees me from the delusion that growth is always visible—that I can always look around and see visible triumph. It allows me to march towards my goals and my dreams, having a renewed relationship with each step. There's a saying that we need to keep our heads in the clouds and our feet on the ground. Life is a continual juggling of extremes, and I think this gets it right. Our strength is in the ability to take those steps—each one a message to the universe that we are stronger than we were yesterday but what makes our journeys truly divine is that they aren't comprised of or built with those steps like a house of cards, where one wrong move or some delay will cause the whole thing to fall, to come crashing down. No, what makes the journey divine is the infinite number of paths that can bring about its materialization. There are no wrong paths. Some arrive sooner; some arrive later. Some mid-journey caused us to realize that the compass wasn't even pointed in the right direction, right? They change what it means to arrive. But the point is, every step is required; every step is a miracle.

However, power is not contained solely in one step but rather in what we choose to make of all the steps combined. The dips, the lows, and the losses only have significance if we give them significance; otherwise, they're just a few stops along the way to something beautiful. So why exhaust energy on data points that haven't arrived yet, on destinations in the future—destinations that we trust ourselves to figure out anyway? Our emphasis should be on the present moment, on gratitude for the fact that we get to wake up and choose the pursuits that we've chosen. And some days, those pursuits will feel like the miracles that they are. We'll see the finish lines, the mountaintops will feel triumphant, and some days, those victories will be hidden in plain view. Still, they are there nonetheless as we make our way into the great unknown that is life, piecing each second, each minute, and each hour together to become the path leading us to where we need to be most.

The Hidden Cost of Waiting

There has to come a time when it's now or never, where you look at your reflection and realize the cost of waiting is far more expensive than the cost of stepping out into the vast unknown. In every journey, that's when life effectively starts. Here's why this is so tricky: what's caught me off guard so many times in my life is the many shapes that waiting takes. See, waiting is not always sitting there and doing nothing—not at all. Sometimes waiting is just the bare minimum; it's moving forward so slightly and so slowly that you can essentially trick yourself into thinking that you're progressing, into thinking you're making it happen. If you really stopped and looked, if you were honest with yourself, and if you really took a second to review and analyze, you'd see that you're leaving almost everything on the table. You're not creating progress; you're dancing with the idea of progress.

Sometimes, waiting can mean just going fast enough not to have to look at the fear you're hiding behind. That's reality, right? I think it's a very normal thing, but I also think life is too short for normalcy. I think we can do better than normal, and I believe with all my heart and soul that the world has for us the spectacular, sitting there on the top shelf, waiting for those who can acquire the self-belief and the awareness to reach out and grab it and how crazy it was to realize that we could have been sitting next to the very thing we'd needed for days, months, and years but never taught ourselves to extend our hands and reach. When I look back, the most important moments in my life were not tangible acquisitions. I see the flashy things that try to capture our attention, right? The money, the condos, even social media growth, business growth—whatever it is you're working towards. Those things are wonderful; they are benchmarks that hopefully align with your North Star, but they are not the difference makers—not at all. Right? They were the byproduct of what really mattered. They weren't the moments that moved the needle.

My greatest moments were mental shifts and cognitive transformations. That's why I do this for a living. I see how much can change when we step back and look at life just a little differently. It was my realizing that I was demanding too little of myself, that the world won't see greatness in me until I see it in me. That shift pushed me to demand more of myself, seek bigger challenges, value my work to a greater extent, charge more for my services, and that mental shift is what made some of those externalities possible. It's realizing that if you want it, more is on the table—that yesterday doesn't define you, that it's never too late to begin again, that everything you need, you have. These are the ideas that truly change lives; they make a difference and if we don't become aware of these things, we leave them in the rearview; we walk right by them.

In other words, the most important moments of my life were when someone or something shook me and effectively said, "Hey, look around you. If this is what you want, fine, enjoy. However, for your information, there is more out there. And if you step up just a little, if you do just a little more, if you pivot and come at this thing a little bit differently, you will further that reach. You'll create another ripple effect that will transform your life." But we must stop and look around.

A good friend of mine—and this is just the other day, right? —we're having lunch, we're talking about marketing and we always joke that marketing is just a part of the business that I don't particularly enjoy—right? Necessary, but not my favorite. Then we're going through different strategies and ideas, and he presents one, and I say something like, "Eh, you know, I don't need to do that. It seems a little over the top and unfiltered." He goes, "Man, you're hurting your reach! What good is that metaphorical restaurant that's not on anyone's radar? You're going to be the best pizza shop that no one knows about." It just kind of hit me, right? It's like, man, I needed to see that differently. Maybe there's room to be a little more aggressive. Additionally, this is one example of many, and not every time is the idea or opportunity the right one or necessary one, right? But at least you stopped, at least you thought about it, and at least you contrasted where you are with the potential upside of doing something differently. That is where we leave opportunity on the table.

We most often, myself included, paint regret as the result of this blatant walking away from something, a deliberate declaration, sort of a, "Oh no, I'm not doing that. No way." And sure, sometimes that's the case. Sometimes, we're aware of our fear and decline to move forward. However, I wonder how often our neglect or refusal is softer, more subtle.

I wonder how much of our regret comes from simply not stopping and looking around, not letting in alternative points of view that challenge us and force us to level up. How much of our regret comes from simply not understanding how short life is and how quickly time passes by? If we don't create some abrupt change in our day-to-day, if we don't manufacture some momentum in our lives—even when it feels less desirable to do so—the ship we need to be on will sail away without us. So, think back to your hardest days, even the ones that took you out, that brought you to your knees, and realize that you survived every single one of them. You have, for years, been acquiring the armor piece by piece to move into something bigger. You've been learning; you've been evolving.

But today, what about sitting down with yourself and having the discussion you don't want to have but need to have? What about asking if it's time to leap where you once stepped, to run where you once walked? What about taking a good look around and asking why you're living in ways that don't serve you, why you're conceding so much of what matters? Again, the evolution you want and need is there; it's always there. And that's the key takeaway here: it will always exist. But the question is, will your commitment to stop, to think, and to reach for it be there?

Years from now, looking back, I think we'll find that our willingness to ask those questions mattered more than we could have ever imagined. That silence often implies the lack of adversity needed to evolve because the reality you want doesn't come to you; you must go to it. And that means reapproaching today's normalcy and comfort, seeing those things for what they are—a continuation of the status quo. Nothing changes until you change. So, take a look around and examine those pillars holding up your worldview—not once but over and over again. And if one, many, or all of them must be knocked down, then so be it. The point here is that you can build.

The point here is that life happens on your terms, whether you realize it or not. Doing nothing is accepting what things are; it's a head nod and a thumbs up to reality as is. Therefore, ask yourself what you want out of life, and if you are missing that mark, tear down what must be torn down. It might be hard now, it might hurt now, it might be uncomfortable now. But when you eventually stand upon an existence that aligns with who you are and what you want, you'll see how necessary it all was, how it was there the whole time. Thank God, you found it within yourself to reach out and take it.

Life is Short: Embrace Every Possibility

It hurts sometimes when you're in that dark place. I need you to hold on. I need you to hold on strong and don't give up. Make an impact in this world. Don't look at it as though it's something that you have to do temporarily, although we know that life is short. Like many people in this world, they didn't realize that the next day, they were going to be diagnosed with cancer. They thought that tomorrow was going to be waiting for them, and they did not wake up. But you are still living. Now, what do you have to do? How are you going to move forward? How are you going to proceed with your life?

Life is not a game; life is living. I say to you right now that you must make it. I say to you right now that you must tell excuses, fear, and doubt that they have no place in your place of business. For this is your life that you are fighting for. This is the life that you are living for. Don't let anyone take away who you are, how true you are, and what you matter in this world to so many other people. Please believe in every possibility that you have and understand that it is not over for you. Maybe you are in a position where you feel that you are broken, or you're feeling that you're going to be broken. But I'm here to let you know, ladies and gentlemen, that you are built to last. I'm here to let you know that you don't have the right to complain anymore. I'm here to let you know that you have to keep on living strong.

You had to experience some things that you did not understand. You had to experience some greatness. You had to experience some weaknesses. You had to experience things that no one could understand. But you are the one that has to be responsible for going through it. You were put on your back, and you probably thought that you couldn't come back. But you did. Dawn is coming, the sun is going to rise, and you will see the light within you. Don't give up on life because once your life is over, you can't come back.

Leave your mark. Help someone. Lift someone when they're down. Be the strength for others when they're weak. And maybe, when you're at the weakest point in your life, someone will lift you. Because we all struggle, no one is immune to it. You must struggle. It is necessary that you feel alone. It would help if you continued to go forward. Nothing can stop this because that light has already been there. That light is embedded in you. That light exists in you. What about the other people out here who can't walk? What about the people out there who can't talk? What about the people out there who are suffering from diseases that cannot be cured? What about you? What are you going to do about the life you have? How are you going to live? How far are you going to go? Run with greatness. Run with a full heart. You've got to be willing to sacrifice. You've got to be willing to hurt. You've got to be willing to yell out whatever it takes. Keep pushing forward. Your life is your life, and you have the right to live it the best way you can.

Yes, it hurts sometimes when you feel alone. It hurts sometimes when you're in that dark place, and you feel no one cares about you. The first thing you've got to realize is that you have to love yourself. It's about self-love. Start understanding that if you're going to do something with your life, you've got to fall in love with yourself again. You've got to stop self-hating. Do something that's going to make you a better person. Make an impact in this world. Don't look at it as though it's something that you have to do temporarily, although we know that life is short. Like many people in this world, they didn't realize that the next day, they were going to be diagnosed with cancer.

They thought that tomorrow was going to be waiting for them, and they did not wake up. But you are still living. Now, what do you have to do? How are you going to move forward? How are you going to proceed with your life? Life is not a game; life is living. There's the good and the bad, and there's definitely the right now. You can't wait for somebody else to make your life better. You've got to make your life better. You've got to focus on you. Now, I'm not saying forget the rest of the people. Still, I'm telling you to get rid of the things that are not making you strong, that are not making you better, that are not making you efficient, that is not putting you in a better place, that are not giving you the strength that you need to keep living the life that you have been given.

Don't give up on life because once your life is over, you can't come back. Leave your mark. Help someone. Lift someone when they're down. Be the strength for others when they're weak. And maybe, when you're at the weakest point in your life, someone will lift you. Because we all struggle, no one is immune to it. So, keep fighting forward. Don't give up. Live. Breathe life. That's what it's about. It's going to hurt sometimes. It's going to get tough. But when it gets tough, you get tough. Just make sure you make your mark. Make sure you make your mark in this world because somebody didn't make it today, but you did. Keep living. Keep living strong. Don't give up. It is not about worrying about what's going to happen tomorrow because guess what? Tomorrow doesn't owe you or me anything. As a matter of fact, tomorrow has already made up its mind.

You have this moment. You can't worry about yesterday because yesterday is not coming back to look for you. Whatever you had the chance to do yesterday won't come back. But you have this moment. You have this chance to do something great with this life that you have been given. You may have been through a lot in your life. You may have been through hell in your life, but hell doesn't own you. Hell did not create you. Life has been given to you by a higher power, something that you need to understand. No matter who you are in this world that we live in today, everyone must struggle. Everyone must suffer. But everybody who is going through something always has a story to tell.

Most people who are successful right now have to go through something to get what they have to this day. Some people are not even willing to hurt. And to feel that. So that they get what they want. But let's go beyond that. What about the other people out here who can't walk? What about the people out there who can't talk? What about the people out there who are suffering from diseases that cannot be cured? What about you? What about you? What are you going to do about the life you have? How are you going to live? How far are you going to go? Do you feel sorry for yourself because you're having a bad day? Do you feel sorry for yourself because you lost your job? Do you feel sorry for yourself because you just feel like you're not having the day that you want to have because the day that you have is not the way you want it to go? Or do you feel that you deserve a pat on your back because you did a good thing?

We all have a responsibility. We all have to be accountable. We all have to put in the work. But don't give up because there's somebody out there right now that is hurting. There's somebody out there right now that is struggling. There's somebody out there right now who's got it a little bit tougher than you do. So why are you going to give up now? For anything that comes your way, you have to be prepared to accept the challenge and go through it. Don't lay on your back. If something's on your chest, get it off. As long as you're breathing, as long as that heart is pumping blood, you're not dead yet. They haven't put rose petals in your box yet. Make sure every breath you take counts for something.

It's time to understand that if you want to get something out of your life, you have to be willing to work for it. How much are you really willing to give? Are you prepared to hurt? Are you prepared to struggle? Because if you're not that person, then lay back down. Stay where you are. Don't move forward; move backwards. But if you are the person that you say you are, we don't have time to wait because time doesn't owe you anything. Time is not thinking about you. Time has already made up its mind. What are you going to do? Who said it's supposed to be easy? It takes grit. It takes tenacity. It takes sacrifice. Stop feeling sorry for yourself. This is not a pity party. But you have the right to celebrate life because no matter if it's good or if it's bad, nothing is greater than living. Because if you're living, there's a possibility to change something, but not just change it—evolve it. Evolve it to something greater. You are being able to take something that may not be anything to others but may mean something to you.

There are so many people in this world who don't believe in you. But while you're sitting around worrying about people believing in you, why don't you focus on believing in yourself? Live. Breathe life. You. That's what it's about. Why do you run? Why are you running? Are you running for a reason? Do you know the purpose behind the run? Do you have enough faith in why you're running? Are you afraid you're going to fall? Do you have enough balance? Are you prepared to test your balance? How fast can you run? Maybe you have to slow down sometimes. Maybe when you cut that corner, you have to understand that when you're turning that corner, there's a unique obstacle that is waiting for you. But are you prepared to run through it? Are you prepared to run fast? Are you prepared to run strong? Do you understand what it means to run?

So many people run away. They run away instead of running forward, instead of running towards something. You may have to take your time and just jog a little bit. But sooner or later, you have to pick up the pace. You have to start moving a little bit faster, and you have to have the desire to run hard. To understand that there's something that has to be done. Don't Run for stats. Don't run for glory. Run because you know it's necessary. But understand that endurance is required. Don't let dead weight slow you down because dead weight is exactly that—it's dead. It has no life, but you have life, and you must continue to push and run as fast as you can. And if you feel that you're getting a little tired, if you feel that you don't have enough left in you, I suggest you push that next button. I suggest you go into that second and third gear. I suggest that you understand that you have to be the one to make it to the finish line. And even when you cross the finish line, prepare yourself for the next race of your life because every day you're racing. Run fast, run strong, run with power, run with greatness, run with a full heart and believe in it. But don't quit. Understand why you're running. If you ever question why you run, believe and know there's a purpose behind everything that you do.

It is time to run for your life. Push in with everything you have inside of you. Run towards an opportunity, run towards a victory, run as hard as you can. You have to understand why you're running. You have to understand the significance of why you're running. Don't run away from the challenges. Please don't run away because it's not going the way you want it to go. Run. Run with a full heart. Run with everything you have in your heart. Get your legs moving and run. Sometimes, you may ask yourself, "How fast can I run? How fast can I get to my destination?" But you also have to understand that when you're running, you have to have in your mind that you have to pace yourself. You have to be able to pay attention when you're running because while you're running, there are going to be obstacles around you. These obstacles are going to be put in place to try to distract you. But you got to keep running. Some days, you're going to be slow, and some days, you just got to be fast. But make sure when you're running, you have your mindset in the right place.

Don't be reckless. Be productive in it and understand that it means something. Recognize your beliefs. Recognize your drive. Don't concern yourself with things that don't concern your best because if you're not giving your best, then the rest will catch up to you. So, stay ahead of the pack and don't slack because it will only push you back. Continue the journey and keep your eyes on the prize. Your rewards are waiting for you. You don't want to be the slowest one on the track, but you have to be the one who thinks.

Please don't take too much time thinking it, but understand that you have to commit to why you're running. Running is good, but you've got to walk a little bit first. You have to walk a little bit so you can understand what's about to happen to you. You have to walk a little bit, so when it's time to put the pedal to the metal, you have your head up, and you're thriving, striking, and moving so fast that nothing around you can stop you. So don't be late for the celebration of your victory because your victory belongs to you, no one else. Take pride in it. Believe in it. Stand on it. Earn it because it's yours. Keep it moving. Be productive. Be powerful. And from the bottom of my heart, run strong, run hard, and conduct your business.

Remember the time when you wanted more? Remember the time when there were people in your life who did not believe in you? Remember the time when you honestly gave up on the possibilities of the uniqueness that you had inside? Remember, there was a time when you complained so much but yet did so little. There comes a point in your life when you must recognize that there's a little bit more that has to be done than just complaining about it. You have to realize that you don't have any other opportunities waiting for you if you're not willing to work for the first opportunity that's been given to you. You don't have a lot of time left, so there's no reason to complain. You're not even in a position to complain. You have to figure out that there has to be another idea about you, and you have to understand that there has to be something even greater and more challenging waiting for you.

If you're not willing to step outside of your comfort zone, if you're not willing to understand the principles and the possibilities that you have within yourself, then everything that you are striving for, everything that you are hungry for, will soon come to an end. Now, I'm not here to preach to you about this. I'm here to let you know that there are things that are going on around you right now that are far greater than you're complaining. You're complaining about so much, but yet you show no action. If you could trade places with someone right now, the person that you're trading places with may have it just a little bit tougher than you have it going on in your life right now. So many people are suffering from so many things in this world at this moment, but yet you're complaining. So many people in this world right now wish they could trade places with you, but yet you're still complaining.

You don't have the right just to give up. You don't have the right just to throw in the towel and say that it's over for you. Ladies and gentlemen, you have to understand that the reason you exist in this world right now is because you have things that must be done, and only certain people are qualified to take it to the level that it needs to be taken to. There should never be a limitation to wherever it is that you are seeking, how far you are willing to travel, and how far you are willing to go.

Sometimes, people tend to get a little lazy. They like to put themselves in this little bitty box and just say that they are okay with where they are. There can never be an "okay" to anything when it comes to life. There should never be a complacent mindset. How do we evolve? How do you evolve? How do you grow? One thing about success: there are going to be many struggles, many challenges, and a lot of things that you may not even understand. But you got to go back to where it started. Remember when you wanted more because you could not satisfy your hunger with negative energy? Being negative doesn't help you to grow. Being doubtful doesn't give you the power that you need. You have to come to a point in your life where you must realize that things are going on that are testing you. Maybe you may be in a position where you feel that you are broken, or you feel that you're going to be broken, but I'm here to let you know, ladies and gentlemen, that you are built to last. I'm here to let you know that you don't have the right to complain anymore. I'm here to let you know that you have to keep on living strong.

I dare you to take a trip to your local hospital. And if you have an opportunity to walk down those corridors and witness so many different people, different age groups, different ethnicities, each one of these individuals is fighting something. They're dealing with some type of sickness, and some of these sicknesses they may not be able to recover from. I dare you to walk down a neighborhood where many people are homeless and have no place to go, no food to eat, and barely even have clothes on their backs. I dare you to realize that maybe you just don't have it so bad after all. Maybe it's time for you to realize and recognize that your troubles are not that bad. Maybe it's time that you realize that you need to get away from the drama that's in your life. Maybe it's time for you to stop chasing misery and start chasing your dreams. Reconnect with yourself because this is not the time for you to be wasting and putting yourself back instead of pushing yourself forward.

Ladies and gentlemen, you have so much to offer, so much to give, and so much to do, but sitting around waiting for it to happen is just going to keep you neutral. You have to electrify the desire that you once had. So, the next time you feel like complaining, you feel like worrying, and you're so concerned about other things that don't necessarily concern you, ask yourself: Is it making you better? Is it taking you higher? Are you going further? Or are you just being complacent? Complacent and complaining and worrying and doing things that are not better for you?

Are you going to realize that maybe just going up that mountain does take a little bit more work than just having something handed to you? Are you going to be that person who realizes that when you get to the top of the mountain, you don't just stop there? You got to figure out another way to go even higher. You have to electrify and get all the things that are necessary within you to start doing the things that you need to do. So, when the time comes, you can kick down that door and move towards the possibility of being the best of who you really are.

Don't lose yourself in things that are not going to give you the strength and the capacity to understand that you matter for something. Don't lose yourself in fear. Don't lose yourself in doubt. Dare yourself to be better. Dare yourself to be unique. Dare yourself to be the best possibility that the world has yet to see. Life—how beautiful it is. How amazing it is to be able to rise in the morning and have that sunshine on your face rather than on your grave. What makes life so unique and so beautiful? It is beautiful because whatever you have that you may be facing, whatever you may be dealing with, life is still good. Life has so many moving parts, but life is always good. Every day is a new day and another opportunity that others may not have. This life that you have been given, this life that you are temporarily holding on to, this life that has been just given to you for only temporary reasons, has more meaning than you can ever imagine. So many people in the world take life for granted instead of realizing that you have to take the opportunity to live it the best way you know how.

Now, on this journey of life, you're going to face a significant number of circumstances and a significant number of challenges. You're going to fall into areas that you cannot understand, and maybe it's not in a position for you to understand at that moment. When you start to feel that you are in a position where you don't love your life, then shame on you because your life is a beautiful thing, and no one deserves to ruin it. No one deserves to control it. No one deserves to steal your joy. Your life is your life. You have the right to live it the best way you can.

You must discipline yourself and take full control and responsibility for the outcome of whatever it is that you are seeking at this moment. There are going to be so many different things that you will embark on. There are going to be so many different things that are going to try to slow you down. There are going to be so many different challenges that you must face. But instead of running away from the challenge, run towards the challenge. Be able to understand that life has meaning, it has reason, and all of these things that you may be thinking are so hard on you—just remember, sometimes you're going to have to go through these changes, these circumstances that put you in a position to make you feel that you're not worthy anymore.

But make no mistake—you are worthy. You were created for something. You weren't created for nothing. Life has a gift, a gift of giving, a gift of receiving, and whether it's good or bad, you've got to make sure you understand that these circumstances and these challenges have to happen in your life. You will come to a point where you may feel that you are in a hopeless situation. You may come to a point in your life when you're at the end of your rope, and the only thing left to do is to climb up because you can only do so much for so long. But make sure you're doing much more instead of doing less. Stop stressing about the things that you cannot control, and start focusing on the things that you have control of. Take control of your life. Take control of the opportunities.

Believe in yourself and know that it is not over for you. So many people out there in this world right now will try to tell you not to be something that you feel in your heart that you want to be. So many people out there right now are miserable, and they'll try their best to take you with them. Do not let misery control your life. Do not let anyone tell you how to live it. Do not let anyone validate your purpose. Do not let anyone validate your destiny. Someone told you a long time ago that you weren't worthy. Someone looked you in the eye and said you weren't going to make it. I say to you right now that you will make it. I say to you right now that you must make it. I say to you right now that you must tell excuses, fear, and doubt that they have no place in your place of business. For this is your life that you are fighting for. This is the life that you are living for. And make no mistake—no one is going to do you better than you.

Don't wait for something to happen. You make it happen. You make it happen for a reason and take full responsibility and control of this thing we call life. When you are doing everything in your power to be the best makeup of yourself, there's always going to be an adversary that's going to try to take that away from you. Now, the best way you can overcome this is by having faith. It doesn't matter what you believe in as long as it's something that's positive and is going to get you through it. A lot of people can't be strong. And I'm not talking about the physical aspect of strength; I'm literally talking about the mental and, of course, spiritual aspect of strength.

Don't let pride confuse your tears. You've got to let that out sometimes. You've got to let it go. When I lost my mom years ago, that was the hardest thing that I had to deal with, and to this day, I still think about that woman who gave me life. And I have my moments when I'm happy about the good times, but I also have my moments when she left this world. But that's just one thing; that's just one circumstance. There are many circumstances I could talk about, but I continue to move on. Everybody gets knocked down. No matter how tough you think you are, you're going to fall. And when you fall, sometimes you fall really hard. But that ground is a hard surface, and I'm going to tell you something—you are not going to move because you're lying on it. So, you need to rise, and you need to rise above it, and you need to start moving. When you get knocked down, how long are you going to stay down? When you lose your job, when you lose that loved one—regardless if it's your husband, your wife, your child, whatever it is—do you have the ability to go through the hurt and the pain of that loss?

Regardless of what you're going through, the best time to know that you are strong is when you're at the weakest point of your life. When you are so far down that hole, you're looking up, and you don't see any light, but you know there's an end to this darkness. That's when you'll find out just how strong you really are.

This is a process, and you have to hurt just a little bit so you can understand what it means to be strong. So don't give up on your hopes. Don't give up on your dreams. Don't give up on yourself. Just keep moving forward. If you think that you're going through something so bad right now, wait until tomorrow. If tomorrow comes for you, look at the person next to you. Look at people all over the world. If you ever come in contact with certain individuals, ask yourself—are they going through a lot more than what I'm going through? Because honestly, there are always going to be people who are going through a lot more than you are going through right now. When you're down, find a way to get up. I've been there. I go through it like anybody else. But I have a job to do in this world, and so do you.

On April 6, 2007, I lost my dad. I lost my mom nine years ago, and I just lost my father. Many people lose things—things that matter to them, things that mean something to them. Recently, I spoke very highly about my father while he was in this world. But now my father is gone, and what hurt me the most is that I didn't have the chance to say goodbye. I didn't have the chance to travel to bury my father because of the crisis that we are facing in our society in this world right now. But yet, I'm here. Yet, I'm still alive. And yet, I still have work to do in this world. Does it hurt? Am I grieving? Do I feel a little bit of despair? Absolutely. Absolutely, I feel that pain. Absolutely, I understand what it means to hurt. Absolutely, I feel like there's nothing else left in me because when I lost my father, a piece of me went with him.

Now, that's not something to just be telling you, I'm telling you the reality of how I feel as a man, as a son, as a father, as a human being. No matter how strong, no matter how tough you think you are, you're going to hurt. You're going to feel that sense of emptiness. You're going to feel that sense of loss. But the best thing about losing is to grow, to feel it, to understand it, and to fight through it. There's nothing; nothing on earth can stop your purpose if you just hold on to it.

So, I live not just for me, not just for my family, not just for the people that look to me, but I do it to honor my parents. It feels not the best of me right now because I don't have that mother to talk to. I don't have that father to talk to or to give advice. It's just me now. The people that mattered in my life, the people that gave me life, are no longer in this world, but they exist in my heart. They give me a reason that they left a legacy for me to carry on. This doesn't mean that it's the end of me. It means that I have work to do. It means that I have to continue to push and go harder and get stronger. It means that I have to stay focused. It means that I have to stay faithful.

To each one of you that is listening to this message, understand the pain, the struggles, and all the things that you felt that are holding you back. It's not going to hold you back for very long because as long as you are alive, you have to continue to move on. You have to continue to live. You can't allow the misery and the hurt and the pain to hold you back to a position where you can't move forward because as long as there's life in that body, you have things that you need to get done.

The reality is we cannot go on forever, but we must go on. We can't live forever, but we must continue to live. We must fight for something. Don't fight for nothing. Live and breathe and fight and believe and understand that it's not over for you. It's not over for you because you are still here. So, make the most of your life. Honor those that are no longer here with us. Make sure you're leaving the mark. Make sure you're leaving the legacy so when your time comes, your legacy can be left to the next generation. So, keep up the good fight. It's not over for me and it shouldn't be over for you. Carry on. Live strong. Keep it moving. And from the bottom of my heart, conduct your business.

Can you see it? Can you see through the darkness? Can you see what's around you? Can you feel the emptiness? Can you feel the loneliness? Darkness is upon you. Darkness surrounds you. The darkness is trying to bring you down. The darkness is trying to take everything from you, but yet you continue to push forward. Can you see it? Do you understand what it means to stand alone? Can you see the light? It builds you up even when you think you're weak. You have a way to be strong. This is not the time to quit. This is not the time to give up. Yes, darkness is upon you, but there will come a time. The sun will shine. Dawn is upon you now. Can you really see the light? Can you really understand the light within you?

Your journey can be seen millions and millions of miles away because you travelled through the darkness. You fought through the darkness. You were down in the darkness. You cried in the darkness. You wandered in the darkness. It is time for you to welcome the light. The emptiness that you are feeling right now is only a temporary match, a temporary thing that is going on inside of you right now. It's only temporary, but it is necessary. You must struggle. It is necessary that you feel alone. You have to continue going forward. Nothing can stop this because that light has already been there. That light is embedded in you. That light exists in you. Dawn is coming. The sun is going to rise, and you will see the light within you. Build yourself up. Strengthen your mind and your body, strengthen your soul, and welcome, and welcome, and welcome the dawn.

Darkness exists at this moment in your life. You're feeling like there's nothing that you can do. You feel that you have no power. You feel that you have no strength, yet you are walking through darkness. Can you see it? Can you really see through the darkness? You are wondering, and you have no idea where to go. You are wondering, and you have no one to turn to. Can you see? Can you see through the darkness? Can you feel your purpose?

Nothing can stop your purpose. Nothing can stop what's meant for you. Nothing around you can stop what's already yours. Your destiny belongs to you. Do you feel it? Do you understand the purpose behind the darkness? It represents something. It serves a purpose. It's an unknown purpose that many of us never would understand. Can you see through the darkness? You travel down this path, you travel down this path of the unknown, and yet you are afraid. You are afraid because you don't understand it. You are afraid because you feel empty. You are afraid because no one is there to help you.

I would like to introduce you to the light, to the dawn, to the beauty, to the understanding, and knowing that this is the joy, this is the joy that you must embrace. This is the moment of happiness without any despair, without any rejections, but an understanding that you made it this far. And no matter what circumstances come your way, the light, the dawn, is upon you. It shines on you. It shines on you because you deserve it. You deserve it because you put so much work in. You've been knocked down. You've been pushed aside. No one believed in you. They rejected you. They said you weren't worthy. Negativity entered into your heart, and you believed it. But then dawn showed up. Dawn showed up. The light showed up and said, "Take my hand. Walk with me. Let me show you the way. Let me show you how far you can go. Let me let you see the beauty within you." Can you see now, with this beautiful bright light that surrounds you, the glow around you? Can you really feel it, not just on the outside but on the inside? Yes, dawn is upon you. The light is upon you.

You made it through the darkness, and now the light shines upon you. There are going to be many other struggles. There are going to be many other challenges, and yes, darkness will come again. But you built up something. You built up a resistance. You built up an opportunity within you. You built up the strength that many others don't have. So regardless of darkness, regardless of light, you keep your head up high, and you keep moving forward. Don't quit. Don't give up on you. Don't give up on the best of you.

This is your time. Through the darkness, you rose above it. You understood what you had to do. You didn't wait for anybody. You didn't wait for anyone to rescue you. You knew what had to be done, and you did it. This is the dawn. This is what you've been chasing. This is the happiness that you were seeking, but it is up to you to continue the journey. You can't stop. The light is within you. Dawn is upon you. It is a beautiful day. It is an amazing day. Can you see it?

It's time to rise and shine. It's time to be about that business. It's time to understand that if you want to get something out of your life, you have to be willing to work for it. I'm talking to the one that wants to go beyond the limit. I'm talking to the one who is willing to work a little bit harder than the next man or the next woman. I'm talking to the one who's been through hell. I'm talking to the one who really wants to take it to that level, yet no one has ever been.

When you step into that room, and into that environment, you have to be hungry enough to eat what is coming your way. You cannot be concerned about what can't be done. You need to be focused on what must be done. If you feel that you are not in a position to do it, then why show up in the first place? You have to understand that it takes grit, passion, and determination to get to the level where you want to be. But you have to understand the difference between levels and going beyond them. You can't stay in one place and expect to get to the next place. You can't look at the sky because, beyond the sky, there's a great big universe.

Now, what are you going to do about it? Are you prepared to push? Are you prepared to work? Are you prepared to dig? You got the fight. You got the push. You have to give everything you have because I tell you this: weakness won't save you. All you need is the power, the strength, and the tenacity to give it everything you got. Have the love for your grit. Have love with every rep that you push out, and understand it is up to you to get the most out of everything that you've worked so hard for.

Now, you've got also to understand this: it isn't going to be easy. It's not going to be a walk in the park. There's always more to give. You've got to be willing to sacrifice. You've got to be willing to hurt. You've got to be willing to yell out. Whatever it takes, keep pushing forward. Don't you give up on your life? Don't you give up on those reps? Don't give up on giving it what it takes to get the most out of yourself.

If you believe in your possibilities, then make it work for you. If you believe that that weight is too heavy, then you won't push it. Suppose you believe that when you're running that mile, and you want to give up, you better find another way and push harder than you've ever pushed. Don't get tired. Don't get weak. Find a way. Make the way. Push your body. Push your mind. Push your soul and give it everything you have because someone else out there may want it a little better than you do.

Now, if you say what you are, then be what you need to be. If you want to get something out of life, then fight for your life. When you're in that gym, find a way to go beyond that limit. Find a way to push your body. It is your body. It is yours. You own it. It belongs to you. The time that you have in this world is only a short time. Make the time count. Make the moment count. Give it something. Feed that body. Build that body. Build that mind. Build that soul and go to work.

Because this is the hour, this is the time. This is it now, and I want to see you working. I want you to dig, feel it, struggle, hurt, bleed, and fight because this is that time. Show the world and show up. And most importantly, do your job and do that business.

This goes out to the firefighters who go through a burning building to help those who can't help themselves. This goes out to the policeman or the policewoman who serves and protects those who can't protect themselves. This goes out to all of those men and women who serve, both far and near, on the front lines. This goes out to our military men and women who give it all. This goes out to those who never made it home. This goes out to the families that will never see their loved ones again.

We must never forget those who put their lives on the line, those who are unselfish and able to contribute what they do each and every day. How can we not recognize them? How can we not recognize what they do? Why does it have to be just one particular day that we honor them? It should never be a one-day thing. Without these people who serve, without these people who give it their all, how can we do what we do? Somebody's got to do the job. They made it up in their minds and their hearts that this must be done, and they are willing to do what is necessary to get the job done.

Think about those kids out there who may not ever see their parents again, whether it was the mother or the father who may have lost their lives in the line of duty. It doesn't matter what you believe in; it doesn't matter how you feel about certain things. Somebody has to be out there. Somebody has to be willing to go through it. Somebody has to be willing to sacrifice. Sometimes, these people never come home. This is the time that we must recognize them. We must recognize those families; they may never see their loved ones again.

Oh yes, it's true: many people put it on the line. Many people get out there every day and do something that has never been done before. Many people out there put it on the line and do something special to help someone else. Why can't we recognize them? No matter where you go, no matter where you may be, someone is out there right now who is doing something far greater, and they're putting so much work in to make a difference in this world. Why can't we honor them? Why can't we honor those servicemen and women?

You have to consider the fact that there are great doctors, great lawyers, great teachers, and great mothers and fathers. There are great people in this world. We all are responsible for one another. We all have a duty. We all have to serve. Whether you wear a uniform or not, you have to serve. Can you be a serviceman? Can you be a servicewoman? Can you serve? Are you prepared to serve? Do you have the ability to serve? Don't make it about yourself. You have a duty. You have a responsibility. They didn't give up; why should you?

Keep moving. Keep believing. We are all one, both far and near. We must serve. So, on this day, we honor the service men and women who put it on the line and who've given their all. If they make it home and have the ability to put their arms around their loved ones, their job is well done. And there will be a new day, and that day starts a new opportunity—a new opportunity to make something else special happen.

Thank you for your service. Thank you for putting it on the line for each day that you go out to do a job that maybe others will never understand, never have the ability to do, or even be able to give the time that you give. For every man and woman who serves, you should always be honored and respected from far and near. You do something that is so great and so special to so many, and sometimes, what you do doesn't get recognized enough.

There should never just be a special day to honor those who serve. Every day should be a special day for you. You are a special individual because you give so much and yet only receive so little. This is the time that you must be recognized for the greatest sacrifices you have made. It would help if you were recognized for your losses, for your struggles, for the things that you have to endure that other will never see.

Today you will be honored, not just this day, but every day for the men and women who serve, for the men and women who give it all, for the men and women that put it on the line and yet do not have the tribute that they deserve. Many people in this world will never understand the pain and the sacrifices that you have given. The fight has always been yours, but this is the time and the moment right now that you must be recognized, that you must understand that you are appreciated.

We should never forget those who have fallen. Never forget those who never made it home. Never forget those who will never have the opportunity to sit at the table and break bread with their loved ones. This is that day to recognize those who serve. Keep up the good fight, everybody. Keep living strong, and never forget our service men and women.

The end of the year is here, and you made it this far. There were good times and bad times, but you are still here. You made it this far because something kept you going, something kept you believing, something helped you understand that the fight was not over yet. This is the year that is soon to come to a close, and there will be a new year, and greater opportunities will be waiting for you. But let's get back to 2024. Let's talk a little bit about what you've been through this year. You had to experience some things that you did not understand. You had to experience some greatness.

You had to experience some weaknesses. You had to experience things that no one could understand, but you are the one who has to be responsible for going through it. You were put on your back, and you probably thought that you couldn't come back, but you did.

Sometimes, you may hear people saying that they're getting old. You're never getting old; you're just getting blessed. If you put your right hand on your heart right now, you can feel that blood pumping. You can feel that purpose. You can feel that reason. You don't have time to complain anymore. Regardless of circumstances, heartaches and pains, joys, and sorrows, you made it. You made it because there was purpose. Purpose doesn't lie; it always, always tells the truth. You just have to understand that this is the time.

As this year comes to a close, 2024 will soon be over. And you have to recognize that there's going to be a new year for you, a new year that is waiting for you. Now, there are no guarantees that tomorrow will be there. There are no guarantees that 2025 will be waiting for you, so make that mark and make that mark right now. Leave the past behind you. Be strong, people. Be strong within yourself, regardless of what you're feeling at this moment right now, regardless of what people may say about you. Be strong because you are a unique creation, and you made it this far because something was meant for you.

We had to experience great losses and witness great victories in 2024. This is the beauty of living, understanding, and knowing that you matter, and the reason that you matter is that you are still here amongst the living. Now, you have to set the new stage, set the new mark, and be greater than you were yesterday. Realize that you are walking above ground for a reason. 2024 may have had its ups and downs, but you did not stay down. You knew what you had to do to get up, so you got up. Maybe that job didn't come through for you in 2024, but 2025 is waiting for you, and if you're able to live and if you're able to push, if you're able to grow, you're going to grow into a better you. Let this be the opportunity of a lifetime. Don't forget: easy was not intended for you or me, for without struggle, how can you build true character?

So maybe you were in a position where you felt broken. But being broken doesn't mean that you can't put it all together again. You must be the architect of your life. Create your own blueprint. Set yourself up, and regardless of whether you fail or succeed, don't give up because if you made it this far, you can definitely go a little bit further. Make 2025 your year. Make 2025 the year that they remember you, that you remember your accomplishments as well as your failures, but don't you ever, ever give up on yourself. This year is coming to an end, and 2025 is right around the corner. Make sure that you are ready. Make sure that you are prepared because 2025 has not been written yet. Just like a book, there are many chapters in the book. What chapter will tell the story about you? What history will you make? What would you leave behind? What legacy would you leave behind? 2025 is the year that we begin a new chapter, a new day, a new year, a new you.

Now, I'm not talking about just the physicality; I'm talking about the mental, the physical, as well as the spiritual, for they are one. They are all connected, but you have to be connected with your self-resilience. You have to be connected with your ideas. You have to be connected with your truth. Don't get disconnected from being who you are. Don't go through 2025 trying to prove something to others who don't believe in you. Whatever happened in the past, let it be. If 2025 is waiting for you, if it's promised to you, make sure you go through 2025 with your head up high and be the best because 2025 will be the year that you will be able to understand it's just another year for you to be better than you was last year. So, make 2025 your year, and let the rest take care of itself.

Life is so short. Life only has a little time, although it will continue to go on. You cannot hold on and think that every day is promised to you. We have all experienced great losses in our life. We have all felt that pain of losing a loved one, someone that we cared about, but yet we're still here, and now we must go on. But what is the example that we're going to leave? What kind of leadership and what kind of leadership qualities do we have? How do we go on? How do we lead the next generation?

Hate is not going to make it work. Being afraid to be truthful about who you are will only limit who you truly are inside. Don't let anyone take that away from you. Don't let anyone take away who you are, how true you are, and what you matter in this world to so many other people. Don't be afraid to be honest. Don't be afraid to be truthful. Don't be afraid to be different. Even being different can be difficult for a lot of people, but I guarantee you this: there is nobody in the world that can do it.

When the time comes, what would you leave behind? What legacy will be left behind to remind others of your greatness, of your losses, of your victories, of your sorrows? This is a short life that we all have, and it's not easy. It's not easy living it every day. It's not easy to go through so many different circumstances and so many different challenges. It's not easy getting that pink slip, knowing that this may be your last day on your job. It's not easy knowing that you may lose your home because you got laid off from your job.

With this type of pain and these different circumstances, many people are always going to come back and say, "Well, that's life." We cannot blame life. It is not life that makes these challenges what they are today. It is the purpose, and purpose never lies. It will always tell you the truth. But why do you exist in this world right now? I need you to hold on. I need you to hold on strong and don't give up. Please believe in every possibility that you have and understand that it is not over for you. I need you to understand life is always going to be good, but always keep in mind that sooner or later, we all have to punch that clock. So, carry on, don't give up, and don't give in. Do the best that you can to have the right attitude to make your existence matter.

Your existence is not by accident; your existence has so much meaning. Are you ready to take on the unknown? Are you prepared for it? You can't even understand, in most cases, how beautiful it is sometimes not even to know what's coming your way. Sometimes, it's not necessary to know everything. Sometimes, it's not necessary to understand everything. But are you ready? Are you ready to embrace the fact that someday, life as you know it, life as I know it, will soon come to an end? Now, what are you going to do about what you're doing with your life right now? See, I talk about life because life is such a great thing. Life is such a beautiful thing. Life has so much universality to it; it is unexplained to some people. It is unimaginable to some people. Sometimes, you may even ask yourself, "I don't even deserve this life." Sometimes, you may even ask yourself, "Why am I suffering so much from this, and that person over there is not suffering as much as I am?"

Ladies and gentlemen, your existence is temporary. It won't last forever. And if you're sitting around wasting it, if you're sitting around being hateful, if you're sitting around being jealous, if you're letting things outside of your circle control your possibilities, your uniqueness, your qualities, your principles—who you really are inside—then what's going to happen next? There will come a time when you leave this world, and they're going to put you in that hole. And guess what, ladies and gentlemen? No one is going to jump in that hole with you. No one is going to jump in there with you and celebrate that death that you just experienced.

Yes, I know it may sound a little harsh; in fact, it may even scare you. But you can't fake this. You can't hide from this. Life is short, and the only thing that's beautiful about it is that when you're living, you have strong possibilities. You have something that you can do to make it impactful for others to see. You can't stop. You can't stop living. You can't stop growing. You can't stop fighting. You have to understand that yesterday, today, and tomorrow are in three different universes, and the only universe you exist in right now is that now, is this moment, is this reality. You can't fix anything that's already been broken. Some things can mend in time, and some things are better off left alone. There are a lot of negative people in this world right now, and there are people who are going to read this book. Some people are read this book right now. Some people are getting this message right now, and yet they'll still find something that is not making them happy. You must make peace within your heart. It would help if you made peace within your spirit. Life is so short.